WITHDRAWN FROM
COLLECTION

GREAT

DISCOVER THE GREAT PLAINS

Series Editor: Richard Edwards, Center for Great Plains Studies

DAN O'BRIEN

PLAINS

Bison

UNIVERSITY OF NEBRASKA PRESS   *Lincoln and London*

A Project of the Center for Great Plains Studies, University of Nebraska

Library of Congress Cataloging-
in-Publication Data
Names: O'Brien, Dan, 1947– author.
Title: Great Plains bison / Dan O'Brien.
Description: Lincoln: University of
Nebraska Press, 2017. | Series: Discover
the Great Plains | Includes index. |
Identifiers: LCCN 2017001111 (print)
LCCN 2017026556 (ebook)
ISBN 9780803285774 (pbk.: alk. paper)
ISBN 9781496203021 (epub)
ISBN 9781496203038 (mobi)
ISBN 9781496203045 (pdf)
Subjects: LCSH: American bison—Great
Plains—History. | Great Plains—History.
Classification: LCC QL737.U53 (ebook)
LCC QL737.U53 O27 2017 (print)
DDC 599.64/3—dc23
LC record available at https://
lccn.loc.gov/2017001111

Set in Garamond Premier by Rachel Gould.
Designed by N. Putens.

This book is dedicated to my wife, Jill O'Brien, and to Richard Edwards, director of the Center for Great Plains Studies, whose persistence saw it through to completion.

CONTENTS

List of Illustrations   *ix*

Introduction   *xi*

Chapter One. The Great Plains: The Lay of the Land   *1*

Chapter Two. Invasion: The First Wave   *15*

Chapter Three. Cleansing the Land: Killing the
Buffalo on the Central and Southern Plains   *26*

Chapter Four. The Empty Land: The
Slaughter Moves North   *37*

Chapter Five. The Old Switcheroo: The Second Wave   *51*

Chapter Six. Penning the Prairie: The Third Wave   *61*

Chapter Seven. The Unintended Consequences
of Technology: The Fourth Wave   *68*

Chapter Eight. The Resistance: Creeping
Back from the Shadows   *81*

Chapter Nine. Legacy: Lessons from the Buffalo   *95*

Appendix: Where to Find Buffalo on the Great Plains   *103*

Bibliography   *105*

Index   *107*

ILLUSTRATIONS

1. Bison movement into the Great Plains, pre-1800s *2*

2. Bison range, circa 1870 *3*

following p. 50

3. *Herd of Bison near Lake Jesse*, John Mix Stanley

4. *Hunting the Buffaloe*, John T. Bowen

5. Shooting buffalo on the line of the
Kansas-Pacific Railroad

6. Soldiers pose with bison heads captured
from poacher Ed Howell

7. *Slaughtered for the Hide*, *Harper's Weekly*

8. Ad, "Millions of acres of Iowa and Nebraska lands for
sale . . . by the Burlington & Missouri River R. R. Co."

9. A pile of bison skulls to be ground for fertilizer

10. Buried machinery in barn lot in Dallas, South Dakota

11. John Jacob Astor

12. Theodore Roosevelt

13. William T. Hornaday

14. William F. "Buffalo Bill" Cody

15. Young bull with older cow

16. Old herd bull with mature horns

17. Cow with "golden" calf

18. Yearling mingling with herd

19. Winter herd watering at the Cheyenne River

20. Buffalo produced for meat in feedlot

This is a short, simple book about a complicated slice of history. It is the story of the relationship between human beings and buffalo. The subject has been dealt with in hundreds of books and scientific papers by noted scholars; some of those sources are listed in the bibliography. Though much of what I have included in this volume came from those sources, I am not an academic. I am a buffalo rancher, a storyteller, and a citizen of the Great Plains.

Great Plains Bison is the story of a place, the Great Plains of North America, and an animal, *Bison bison bison*, the dominant species on those plains for most of the last eight thousand years. Of course, *buffalo* is a popular misnomer. The buffalo of the North American plains are more properly called bison, and they have two close cousins—the European wisent (*Bison bison bonasua*) and the North American wood buffalo (*Bison bison athabascae*). All three subspecies have suffered huge declines in numbers as humans have prospered, but the history of the plains buffalo of North America is the most dramatic because their population was so enormous and their decline so precipitous.

I first saw the Great Plains sixty years ago and have lived on them, within sight of the Black Hills, for forty-five. I have traveled the length and breadth of the Great Plains and have found that it is a deceptively intricate place. Every watershed has its idiosyncrasies: different grasses, birds, and mammals. The wind and weather sweep the sky in different ways. The seasons wear different masks, and the history has quirks and foggy spots. Now, my wife and I live along the Cheyenne River, our land is surrounded by the Buffalo Gap National Grasslands and borders the Badlands National Park and the Pine Ridge Indian Reservation, and our livelihood comes mostly from raising buffalo. Because our neighbors, the Lakota people, consider buffalo a nation in themselves, I would have preferred to capitalize the word *buffalo* throughout this book—the same as I would *Irish*, *French*, *Armenian*, or *Swede*. But the editing standards defined in the *Chicago Manual of Style* will not allow such a deviation from Eurocentric thinking. So, while *buffalo* must be printed in lowercase, I will refer to Native Americans as Indians, because that is what they call themselves.

Our land is a hard place to know because its most important characteristics can be subtle. Most people are only passing through, and even those of us who have chosen it as a home begin to really know it only when we are approaching the age of uselessness. Last spring was the wettest year that anyone can remember. At night the unfamiliar song of chorus frogs pulsed like a billion descending locust and one of our pastures grew up thick with a species of grass I had never seen before. Apparently the frogs and the seeds had laid there waiting for years or decades, which only proves that the span of a man's life is not nearly long enough to understand much. Even the science books—botany, biology, hydrology, geology, ethnology, and meteorology—do not impart enough to explain the Great Plains.

I have found, ironically, that when I want the truth of a subject—not just the facts—it's best to turn to poetry or fiction. But in the case of the Great Plains, most of the stories have been usurped by political historians or the creators of entertainment and, fascinating as those takes on Great Plains stories can be, they bear little resemblance to the reality of this place. The Great Plains are a favorite stopover for literary carpetbaggers who rush back to the coasts after a few days or weeks with what they imagine is the story of the place. Because the sunsets and sunrises are spectacular and the people are colorful and often upbeat, such writers seldom realize how truly sad this ecosystem is. It is one of the most exploited and least protected landscapes in the world. The historians have part of the story, the scientists, homesteaders, and Indians have part, but only the buffalo know the whole story.

In the spring of 2016 the buffalo became the national mammal of the United States. It follows that a book about buffalo should try to explain what this iconic and greatly loved animal has witnessed in its eight thousand years on the Great Plains. From the buffalo's ancestors who crossed the Bering land bridge long before our own ancestors to the buffalo that graze our pastures here on the Cheyenne River Ranch, they alone have seen it all. Anyone who has been on the Great Plains, has spent hours alone with a herd of buffalo, and has looked into their dark, otherworldly eyes has been forever changed. It is impossible to forget those eyes. There is no deeper well of wisdom.

GREAT PLAINS BISON

CHAPTER ONE

The Great Plains

The Lay of the Land

When Americans dream there is an enormous blue sky and grasslands rolling to a distant horizon. There is a steady breeze bringing the scent of possibilities. There are no restraints, no boundaries, and no limits. When Americans dream, we dream like buffalo. It is as if we can stand in their skins, stare with their beguiling dark eyes, and let the rare prairie rains drip benignly from our noble goatees. We imagine ourselves as country boys or strong young women with long, smooth muscles, solid bodies, and steady hands. We feel a kind of innocence, tempered with confidence and power. There is the thousand-yard stare of wisdom, patience, and endurance. When we dream like buffalo we can imagine ourselves as the center of the world.

To the culture that came before us buffalo were, in fact, the center of their world. The highly mobile, equestrian Plains Indians relied on the buffalo for everything that made life possible. They believed that they were related to buffalo. The stories that were told as lessons to the children often involved interaction between buffalo and people: the gods had made them from the same dirt, people and buffalo could easily converse, they could change places, and they helped each other survive on the sometimes hostile Great Plains. For most of the

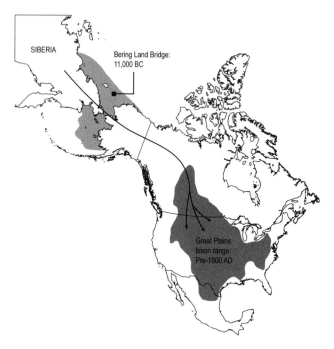

1. Bison movement into the Great Plains, pre-1800s. Map created by Katie Nieland.

history of buffalo, among almost all peoples, there has been reverence, respect, and deep affection for the animal.

Yet there is something sad about buffalo. At times they have been misunderstood, exploited, commoditized, and abused. Even their identity has been hijacked by a succession of cultures. They are the animal with two names, buffalo and bison. The first name stems from the confusion of the Europeans who landed their boats on the eastern shore of North America in the sixteenth century. Those crude men thought they were on a different continent and that the large, shaggy animals they found were a variant of the water buffalo they knew from Asia

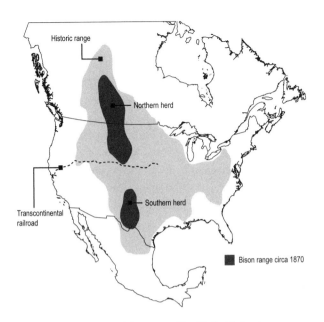

Historic range

Northern herd

Transcontinental
railroad

Southern herd

Bison range circa 1870

2. Bison range, circa 1870. Map created by Katie Nieland.

or the Cape buffalo they had heard of in Africa. It was not until centuries later that European taxonomists decided the American bovine was a unique specie and named it bison. A better name might be Tatonka, the name given by the horse people of the Great Plains. But even that name came late in the reign of buffalo on the North American continent.

The first buffalo were native to what is now Asia and Europe and crossed into North America on the Bering land bridge. It is hard for us to imagine how different the world was back then—the continents all ajar, molten rock surging up from below, and sea levels rising and falling as a result of ice caps varying in thickness from mere ice sheets to gigantic water repositories many miles thick. But there was a window of perhaps fifty thousand years when all sorts of creatures made the trek across the land bridge. Hundreds, perhaps thousands of species moved. They traveled both ways—the ancestors of animals like camels, cheetahs, and horses heading for Asia, and mammoths, buffalo, and early humans coming to North America.

But long before this great intercontinental migration of animals, the continents themselves were migrating. For hundreds of millions of years the crust of Earth twisted and turned, rose and fell tens of thousands of feet. Water surged into the gaps and lowlands, bringing tiny sea creatures; when they died, they formed layer after layer of sediment that settled and turned to rock only to be pitched and pushed up for more millions of years. The effect was a great churning and mixing of Earth's surface that, as the climate became less hostile to life, formed a mosaic of different surfaces where species of every sort might gain toeholds. The first species to appear on the North American continent were the algae that would eventually evolve into ferns and then into plants that would support the animals that were evolving ways to utilize terrestrial vegetation.

After the great geologic upheavals, the future home of the buffalo found itself in the middle of the North American continent, bordered on the west by the towering Rocky Mountains and on the east by a lowland falling off to the sea. By the time the geography and climate began to settle, the midcontinent was a dry, windy place. Trees claimed the lowlands to the east but remained rare on the Great Plains, where grasses reigned. When humans finally came along and needed a name for the huge expanse, they settled on another misnomer, Great Plains. The Great Plains are certainly great: over two thousand miles by five hundred miles—the largest ecotype in North America. But they only look like plains: they were almost never flat. In fact, the Great Plains vary in elevation by thousands of feet. There are millions and millions of depressions, cuts, watercourses, hills, ridges, buttes, and small mountain ranges—every one a potential niche for the animals that had already begun their march across the land bridge.

Many Old World mammals, like mammoths, three-toed sloths, and the modern buffalo's big, slow cousins (*Bison latiforons*), were trapped in the changing climate of North America and killed off by nomadic Asian hunters. The modern buffalo, however, evolved into an animal too fast and mobile to be easily hunted. Early Americans, later to become Indians, were still centuries away from the grand alliance with the modern horse, and distances across the grasslands were too great for easy pedestrian hunting. The mobile buffalo could not be reliably killed with clubs and stones. As a result, they got the chance to multiply and spread out across these new grasslands. Food for grass-eating animals was everywhere, and buffalo evolved to move at a pace that far outstripped humans.

Buffalo, however, were tame enough that occasionally men, on foot, with Stone Age tools were able to kill a few of them as a very nutritious supplement to their diet of foods gathered from the river bottoms. At times they stalked and killed the buffalo with spears. These encounters were likely in the transition zones between riparian areas, where the humans lived, and the vast sea of grass that the buffalo preferred. Later the early Americans' ingenuity led them to select special landscapes where buffalo could be herded into rough corrals for slaughter or run over cliffs to die by the many dozens a hundred feet below. Though buffalo are basically docile animals, to this day they do not like to be corralled and they have an uncanny ability to remember the natural features of the land that might give them escape routes. They remember the lay of the land so well that it is difficult to picture a herd of buffalo being pushed over a cliff or into a corral, but archeological evidence leaves little doubt that this happened on occasion. To construct from gathered wood and rock a corral that would hold a group of crazed, leaping, and running buffalo is hard to imagine. Such hunts would have required tremendous coordination and focus. It would have taken weeks or months of labor and lots of luck to make one successful. Yet scattered over the Great Plains there are remnants of such hunts in the form of piles of buffalo bones marked with the signs of carnage.

These hunt sites were used occasionally for thousands of years, but only if a herd of buffalo was in the right place, if a band of hunters was near, if the wind was blowing from the right direction. In some cases, Indians probably set fires in the fall of the year, when the grass was dry, in hopes that the fresh, new grass of spring would attract the herds. Still there was a lot that could go wrong, and many hunts were likely not successful. When a person visits one of these sites, the tendency is to look down at the layers of bones that represent dozens or even hundreds of buffalo per year and think, "My God, look at all these buffalo." But it is important to realize that during the time these sites were used perhaps five million buffalo were born every year. If you raise your eyes from the bones and look at the miles of grass in every direction, you realize that this method of hunting buffalo was of little consequence.

It is popular to glorify the land ethic of Native Americans by saying that they used all the parts of the buffalo and to negatively compare the nineteenth-century bloodbaths where Europeans killed for a few body parts and wasted the rest. But if you can imagine a hot July afternoon in eastern Montana with a hundred dead and dying buffalo laying at the bottom of a cliff you will realize that this notion is pure romanticism. We want to believe that all the buffalo that went over the cliff died instantly upon impact, but they did not. Buffalo can be very tough. Most that went over the cliff would likely live to run on three legs, or even two, just over the hill or for many miles, were they could die from blood loss or starvation, or the wolves that would have begun to gather when the first screams of agony began.

On a warm day, a dead buffalo will bloat and putrefy in a few hours. Imagine further a whole village of early Americans—men, women, and children—without steel knives and with horse-power still a century in their future, struggling to bludgeon the fatally wounded and then process carcasses. A little putrefaction probably didn't bother them but still, by our standards, most of the buffalo would have been wasted. But of course, that is an ethnocentric accounting of this scene. In fact, if the entire ecosystem is considered, nothing is wasted. On the Great Plains, as in any ecosystem, there are layers of species, from predatory birds to microbes waiting to take their turn. Eagles and vultures would have been circling above the buffalo slaughter. Wolves, coyotes, and foxes would have been sitting on the surrounding ridges, waiting patiently. Magpies and jays would have flut-tered around the humans as they worked. When night came, the cats would slip silently to the outlying carcasses. Rodents would begin to move, and the smell of rot would announce the activity of bacteria and fungi. Even today, in an ecosystem denuded of many of its parts, a buffalo carcass can be reduced to nothing but dry bones in a few days. In truth, those early American hunters had nearly no impact on the ecosystem of the Great Plains or the buffalo as a species. The Great Plains were too vast and the buffalo were too numerous.

Hernán Cortés, during his conquest of the Aztec Empire of Montezuma in 1521, was allegedly the first European to see a buffalo. A Spanish historian claimed that Cortés and his men had seen that first buffalo in a zoo in Montezuma's capital near present-day Mexico City. One of Montezuma's subjects likely captured it somewhere north of the Aztec capital and brought it to the ruler as some sort of tribute. It was not until Álvar Núñez Cabeza de Vaca and Francisco Vázquez de Coronado reached what is now Texas that they began to see buffalo in any numbers. Like Cortés, their focus was on finding gold, so they didn't say much about buffalo in their accounts, except that they were excellent for eating.

Though the early Spanish found what they thought were a lot of buffalo, their activities only skirted the Great Plains, the mother lode of the world's buffalo. Even Coronado's penetration of what is now Kansas seems to have missed the truly enormous herds found along the Arkansas River three centuries later.

Father Louis Hennepin, a French missionary, was reported to be the first Frenchman to see a buffalo. In 1679 he sailed from Quebec City to the southwest corner of the Great Lakes, where he found a buffalo mired in the mud on one of the prairie openings in the savannas of Illinois. He took the time to study the animal before he shot and ate it. A handful of buffalo were seen in Virginia and North Carolina in the early 1700s. They were regularly killed by colonists even though they were described as "so gentle and undisturbed" that they could nearly be petted. By 1760 almost all of the wandering buffalo along the East Coast had been killed by the new Americans.

West of the Appalachian Mountains there were a few more buffalo, and adventurers like Daniel Boone preyed on groups of up to a thousand animals. After the American Revolution, when the "western lands" that ended at the Mississippi River were officially opened to settlement, the remaining buffalo were quickly killed. The scattered eastern survivors were picked off in Ohio and Indiana. Reportedly, the last buffalo east of the Mississippi River was killed in Wisconsin by two Sioux Indians in 1832.

Those buffalo that were early casualties of the westward expansion of Europeans were stragglers from the heart of their kingdom. Once they crossed the Mississippi, Europeans began to understand the magnitude of that kingdom. The European mind was about to get a New World lesson in scale.

The land from the Mississippi River east to the Atlantic Ocean was mostly forested. As Euro-Americans cleared the trees for their farms and cities, they found rich, dark soil built up over centuries by accumulating humus from the litter created by those well-watered forests. But beyond the Mississippi the world changed: here, soils were made of different geological stuff and, though fertile, much of it was thin and dry. In North America the weather moves generally from west to east. Moisture-laden clouds move from the Pacific Ocean toward the Atlantic. But the Rocky Mountains are thousands of feet higher than the land on either side so the clouds have to rise up to get over them. When the air rises to clear the mountains, it cools and water vapor condenses out as rain or snow. By the time that air reaches the Great Plains, the water has been wrung out and there is little moisture left to fall on the kingdom of the buffalo. This is a curse for modern crop farmers but the buffalo evolved strategies for not only surviving the lack of moisture on the Great Plains but thriving in numbers nearly beyond the imagination of man.

The evolutionary plan of plants, when faced with the Great Plains, was something along the lines of, "What doesn't kill you makes you stronger." Plants adapted to the lack of rainfall, temperature extremes, wind, and fire. What millions of years of evolution built for the Great Plains is a group of short plants that can reproduce both by seeds and by root-runners sent out along the ground. The foliage that is visible is only a small part of the plant and dies back every winter. Most of the plant is safely below ground in the form of an extensive root system that moves elements like carbon, nitrogen, phosphorous, and oxygen back and forth from the air to the earth. In good years, prairies can produce tons of grass and other plants per acre. As a result, the ancestors of buffalo evolved to eat, almost exclusively, those tons of forage. Even during winter, when plants are dead and dry, prairie grasses maintain most of their nutrition. When cut and stacked or baled, we call it hay. But for tens of thousands of years before machines, it was standing "hay." A buffalo can eat four of five tons of dry grass per winter, and luckily for the buffalo, many hundreds of millions of tons grew on the Great Plains each year. It was a great place to be a buffalo.

For centuries before Euro-Americans had any significant presence on the Great Plains there were rumors about what lay beyond the Mississippi River. Some thought that the Pacific Ocean was just over the horizon. There were stories of cannibalistic Indians and horrible monsters, sand dunes, and glacier-topped mountains. Indians told of boiling hot springs and treeless grasslands that took weeks to cross. Early French trappers claimed that there were more buffalo than a person could count. Over the centuries the entire Great Plains area was claimed by various European nations, and trappers and traders made various forays onto the grasslands, but generally the area was ignored.

It was not until 1803, when the United States bought a giant swath of land west of the Mississippi River from France, that better organized and equipped expeditions were dispatched to find out what was really out there. The Indians were generally not cannibals and there were no real monsters. There were a few sand dunes and huge mountains with glaciers on top. There were boiling hot springs and lots of immense prairies. And there were indeed more buffalo than a person could count.

The Lewis and Clark expedition set out, under orders from Thomas Jefferson, a year after the land was purchased in 1803. There is little doubt that some of the thirty-three men in the group had seen buffalo before, but all were excited to see their first buffalo in the new territory. They had not traveled far up the Missouri River from their starting point on the Mississippi near Saint Louis when they saw a herd they believed was three thousand strong. Buffalo continued to be sighted from their boats on the Missouri River and on side expeditions onto the higher ground. In fact, herds numbering in the hundreds and even thousands became a common sight during the expedition. The men ate, and greatly enjoyed, buffalo meat almost constantly until they reached the Rocky Mountains and left the plains. On the return trip to Saint Louis, they found even more buffalo all the way through what is now Montana, North Dakota, and into South Dakota, where, according to the Lewis and Clark journals, they "discovered more than we had ever seen before at one time: and if it be not impossible to calculate the moving multitude, which the whole plains [contains], we are convinced that twenty thousand would be no exaggerated number."

As other explorers, trappers, and settlers began to move across the Great Plains they reported herds of similar size. From above the Canadian line nearly to Mexico, buffalo seemed to be everywhere Euro-Americans looked. Of course, the Indians who lived on the Great Plains had already created a culture built around horses introduced by the Spanish and the omnipotent buffalo. They knew that in one season or another, buffalo could be seen from almost any high ground on the Great Plains. Because of the nature of Plains Indian culture there was probably little effort put forth by Native Americans to quantify the population of buffalo on the Great Plains. But Euro-Americans wanted numbers.

By the mid-1880s reports of tens of thousands of buffalo, even hundreds of thousands, were coming in from the southern plains. There were stories claiming sights of thousands of buffalo crossing rivers. People swore that for as far a person could see the prairie was covered with brown fur and black horns. Others had ridden a horse for days without being out of sight of buffalo. Horace Greeley, editor of the *New York Tribune*, speculated that there were once five million buffalo on the Great Plains. The buffalo hunter Robert Wright said twenty-five million. Ernest Thompson Seton, a respected naturalist, came up with an estimate of seventy-five million. General Philip Sheridan, the Civil War hero and Indian fighter, had seen a lot of buffalo during his escapades on the Great Plains and made a stab at calculating the total: one hundred million.

Memoirs and local history books are filled with impressions of buffalo numbers on the plains drained by the Missouri. In *Hunting and Trading on the Great Plains, 1859–1875*, James Mead recalls the fall of 1860 along one of the western tributaries of the Missouri:

> In the fall the first wave of returning buffalo stopped in the valley and had a regular spell in the tall grass and weeds. They were almost as tame as domestic cattle; fat and fine. They kept coming until the valley was full before they crossed the river. In a week's time nearly all the grass in the country was eaten off close to the ground. Then, for the next three weeks, there was a steady wave of buffalo passing on to the south, day and night. The unceasing roar continued and, when their myriads had passed, the surface of the earth was worn like a road cut into innumerable parallel paths. Three weeks later I went forty miles west, and found vast herds of buffalo still passing south.

Modern estimates put the number around thirty-five million, but we will never know the actual number of buffalo on the Great Plains before Euro-Americans came on the scene. We know very little about the life history of wild buffalo because no one really studied them until the huge herds—the truly wild buffalo—were gone. In the early nineteenth century buffalo were scattered from the Mississippi River to the Rocky Mountains—from Mexico up and into Canada. Buffalo came together in big herds during the summer breeding season, and they usually split up into smaller herds for the rest of the year. They seemed to be always in transit, perhaps searching for the best grazing, but often moving through grass that appeared to be more than adequate. If deep snow covered the grass they were likely to move to where grasses were more accessible, but bad weather, in itself, never seemed to be the reason for their movement. Perhaps it was as simple as the first line of the poem by Dr. Brewster M. Higley that became the unofficial anthem of the American West: "Oh give me a home, where the buffalo roam."

On our ranch in South Dakota we notice the same thing in miniature. A herd of several hundred buffalo might spend a day or two on a particular slope or broad meadow—grazing, resting, sleeping, milling around, and preforming the rituals of the breeding season—until it seems that they will be there forever. Then, for a reason that humans can only guess at, an old cow will stand up, stretch, and strike out—with her calf at her flank. A cousin and her calf will follow and soon the whole herd is gone, swallowed by the enormity of the plains. They may walk, or lope, for miles before they settle again in a completely different area, where they may stay for a few hours or another couple days. But soon, they will be on the move again.

This movement is what makes them buffalo. And it is moving buffalo that made the Great Plains what they are, since the hooves of buffalo massage the prairies in a way that stimulates the growth of grass. Architects and builders call the wedge-shaped stone placed at the apex of a masonry arch a keystone. It is the keystone that locks all the pieces together and gives the arch strength enough to endure. Biologists use the same term to describe a species that plays a similarly unique and crucial role in the way an ecosystem functions. Without its keystone species, an ecosystem would be dramatically different or cease to exist altogether. Buffalo are such a species. But not just the buffalo: free-moving buffalo. The interplay between the great herds of America's largest animal and every other species, from soil microbes to soaring eagles, formed the unique ecosystem of the Great Plains. Without the movement and grazing of tens of millions of buffalo, the Great Plains would have been something very different from what Euro-Americans found when they pushed out from the forests of eastern America. As soon as the number of buffalo began to diminish and their movement began to slow, the Great Plains began to change.

The Great Plains have always been changing, but the time it took to shift from buffalo dominance to human dominance was short and represents an anomaly when viewed in the sweep of history. The Indians of the Great Plains buffalo culture, who believed they were related to buffalo, said that the reason for the tremendous shift in balance was the loss of respect by the two-legged branch of the buffalo family for the four-legged branch. Western scholars might see it as the tragic flaw of humanity as expressed in the myth of Cain and Abel. Both views may be right. Certainly a violent tragedy of betrayal occurred in the nineteenth century. But the nightmare continues. The drama is still being played out on one of the world's largest stages, and through it all, the buffalo have been both actors and audience.

CHAPTER TWO

Invasion

The First Wave

Early varieties of buffalo were on the North American continent long before human beings crossed the temporary land bridge over the Bering Strait. Modern plains buffalo evolved from these early versions when humans were still a very rare species on the continent, but in a sense, our species developed together. Humans exerted some of the evolutionary pressure that made the buffalo the animal that Europeans found when they came to the continent in the sixteenth century: a large, highly mobile, grasslands animal with a tremendous instinct to form and stay in huge herds. But the few humans that were on the continent early had limited technology that restricted them to river bottoms and coastal forests, so it was primarily large predators and a changing climate that drove buffalo to the vast grasslands in the center of the continent. In fact, among the thousands of generations of buffalo that had lived on the North American continent before Columbus, very few had ever seen a human being. The invasion of Europeans would rapidly change all that.

Soon after the Lewis and Clark expedition, hundreds of boats full of hunters and trappers began ascending the Missouri, but except for a fat cow or two shot from the river for food, they left the buffalo alone. Many of these men were French, and though they all agreed that the taste of American buffalo was superior to anything they had eaten in their home country, they took only what they needed for sustenance. They were not after buffalo, and unlike the Spaniards to the south, they were not after gold. The first men to ascend the Missouri River en masse were after beaver.

Europeans had been hunting beaver since they landed on the eastern shore. At first they traded iron tools for beaver and other pelts to use as winter clothing in this new, harsh country, but they soon began to ship a few pelts back to Holland, France, and England. Felt hats were in style in Europe, and beaver fur made the very best hats. By the mid-1600s the Dutch began an international trade in beaver skins. The pelts were shipped to Europe at tremendous profit, and this business model spread westward with settlement. By the time beaver trappers and traders found the arteries of the Great Plains, the rivers of the east had been ravaged and their beaver were nearly extinct. But beaver-felt hats were still in style in London, Amsterdam, and Paris, so the hunt for healthy beaver populations pushed into the buffalo kingdom.

For hundreds of years, over hundreds of miles, and especially after the horse returned to North America in the form of the supersized Spanish military mounts, there had been commerce between the Indian tribes. Flint had been traded for turquois. Dried meat for corn. Marine shells for leather goods. Centers had been established for this trade, and they became important meeting places for the tribes. Great Plains Indians were not strangers to the concept of trade, and the Europeans who crept up the rivers of the Great Plains in the nineteenth century were masters of the art. It was only a question of establishing a presence in the vicinity of a historic Indian trade center and notifying the locals that beaver pelts could be traded for iron kettles, knives, axe heads, awls, jewelry, cloth, beads, firearms, ammunition, or alcohol. The Great Plains Indians had never seen such things, and so all the traders had to do was wait for the beaver pelts to come rolling in.

In those days watercourses ran pure and cold and nearly every fragment of moving water held beaver. The Indians knew all the beaver houses and dams, and though they had used the pelts only for special decorative fur work in the past, they quickly figured out how to kill them in quantity. In the beginning they were driven by desire to own an iron knife, a stewpot, or a length of red cloth, and at first it was easy to encourage the Indians to do the trapping and preparation of the hides.

The long-standing trade economies of the Great Plains were changed immensely not only in terms of what was being traded and the sheer size of the trade but also in the ramifications of that trade on the cultures and ecosystems of the Great Plains. Trade in articles made of iron propelled the Indians from the Stone Age to the Iron Age in a single century. But in every bright, red, metaphoric apple that the Europeans brought to the Indians there seemed to be a worm. It is a recurring theme in the concept of progress.

This new brand of trade was a revolution that initially, and temporarily, improved the living conditions of most Indians. Household goods like kettles and steel knives were tremendous improvements over hot rocks dropped into a buffalo-hide pouch and flint tools. But, as in the case of the trade muskets that the Indians prized above almost anything else, trade with Europeans would eventually cause as much trouble as it did good. Whiskey proved to be a pitfall for most tribes and an irresistible trade item that deprived the Indians of their pelts and hides and left them with ensuing social decay. Many of the changes that came with European trade were not obvious until it was far too late. The breakdown of Indian culture was one insidious outcome of economic intercourse with the Europeans, but far more sinister were the diseases that ran ahead of the Europeans and decimated native culture to the point that, when Europeans finally appeared in the flesh, the civilizations they encountered were mere shadows of what they had been. Given Indians' lack of resistance to such diseases as smallpox, measles, bubonic plague, influenza, typhus, syphilis, and scarlet fever, some scientists assume a death rate of 95 percent where Indians came into contact with the bacteria and viruses of Europe and Africa—snaking ahead of the actual conquest via innocent individuals who passed between tribes. At even a fraction of that rate, the effects would have been devastating.

There is no way of knowing if the buffalo nation suffered similar germ-driven devastation, but in Ballard C. Campbell's *Disasters, Accidents, and Crises in American History* we are told that the colonists not only carried diseases but also brought livestock that carried diseases too. It is likely that buffalo were infected by the diseases of colonists' domestic animals and the vermin that came with them.

Indeed, anthropologists have suspected for decades that Hernando de Soto's expedition out of Florida in 1539, in addition to the rape, torture, enslavement, and murder of countless Indians, may well have been responsible for the near complete collapse of Indian culture in what is now eastern Arkansas and beyond. A population of perhaps two hundred thousand was reduced to about eighty-five hundred. De Soto accomplished this feat not by force of arms but by bringing European pigs with him. Pigs could have easily carried the pathogens for smallpox and measles in a form that was benign to de Soto's men, who were used to them, but cataclysmic to American Indians. Almost every European expedition herded hundreds of domestic animals ahead of them. The damage done by these four-legged intruders to the buffalo will never be known.

In the early 1800s men like John Jacob Astor, William H. Ashley, Pierre Chouteau, and Manuel Lisa made enormous profits by outfitting traders who set up forts along the rivers running into the Missouri. But the trade became more difficult once Indian households accumulated the basic iron tools that they needed. The market softened, and the Indians began to understand that the pelts were worth more than they were getting from traders. They began to demand more luxuries for their services—whiskey and muskets became standard trading fare and the inevitable conflict associated with trade began to escalate.

Drunk and armed, the Indians became much more difficult to work with and the traders turned to hiring their own men to do the trapping. The now-mythical hero called (often erroneously) the mountain man was born, and thousands were sent out to penetrate the interior of the Great Plains in search of beaver. Along with the mountain man and the fur trading companies came the concept of all-out, mortal competition to control the fur trade on the Great Plains. Indians, who had long squabbled with other tribes over hunting grounds, now learned to fight viciously. With the help of trade muskets and horses, the Great Plains entered an era of violence never before dreamed of.

The mountain men, protected by superior firearms, systematically trapped the beaver out of the Great Plains streams as they moved from the plains to the mountains. They also trapped river otter, mink, martin, and a host of other fur-bearing mammals for processing and export to the East Coast and on to Europe to be turned into clothing and felt hats. But, though they used buffalo robes for their own winter clothing and shelter, they killed relatively few buffalo for profit. There are many reports of trappers being closely observed by buffalo who stood along the frosty riverbanks and watched the trappers wading in the icy water to check their beaver traps, but trappers mostly left the bison alone.

By the 1840s the beaver of the Great Plains began to give out. In conjunction with other economic forces the decline in the availability of beaver pelts encouraged a swing toward silk as the main raw material for fashionable hats. Beaver soon became worthless, and thousands of traders, mountain men, and Indians were out of work. But the keystone was still in place. Buffalo were still moving across the plains pretty much as they had always done. But, even after the near extinction of their beaver brothers and sisters, the buffalo had no way of knowing that economic pressures halfway around the world were driving Europeans to covet their home, develop ways to use their bodies in industry, and plan their elimination.

About the time that beavers disappeared from most of the rivers and streams of the Louisiana Territory, the United States went to war with Mexico. Victory was a certainty. The land that was eventually ceded to the United States included the last, small portion of the Great Plains. By 1848 the entire Great Plains belonged to the United States and the political question of the day was whether the new states that would be created from all that land would allow slavery or not.

The turmoil in the U.S. Congress generated a third party to oppose the two mainstream parties. The Free Soil Party emerged from the fray in 1848 and was made up mostly of antislavery Republicans and Democrats from the northern states. Martin Van Buren, who had been the president of the United States ten years before as a Democrat, was the Free Soil presidential candidate in 1848. In that campaign he not only insisted that the new states would come in as non-slave states but also suggested a homestead law that would basically divide up the land that belonged to the Indians and the buffalo and give it to U.S. citizens. It would take another fourteen years for this idea to become popular, but on January 1, 1863, the same day that the Emancipation Proclamation was signed by Abraham Lincoln, the Homestead Act of 1862 became law. The act laid out a procedure that would transfer ownership of 160 acres of the Great Plains from the U.S. government to any qualified person. So, on the same day that three million black men and women gained their freedom, perhaps thirty-five million buffalo lost theirs.

In the next forty years eighty million acres would be transformed from one functioning, sustainable ecosystem to many thousands of nonsensical political units operated by men with little experience in land management and almost no real knowledge of the Great Plains. The Homestead Act of 1862 was an ill-advised action by a government obsessed with expansion and the belief that a republic is best served by free, non-slave-owning men, each cultivating his own small piece of land. After the American Revolution, Thomas Jefferson had championed this social structure with regard to the American South, trying to find a democratic solution to the disparity in wealth between the upper-class tobacco and cotton plantation owners and common men who worked much smaller plots of land. In typical idealistic fashion, Jefferson praised such small farmers as ideal republicans. Ironically, he called them yeoman farmers, a term borrowed from England and referring to servants of the king. So powerful was the idea that lower-class Americans could and should become landowners that Civil War–era Americans were willing to bet the future stability of the entire western half of their new nation on a plan devised for the southern United States, where the rainfall was three or four times that of the Great Plains and where it almost never snowed.

The concept of the yeoman farmer depended upon fertility and rainfall like that in Europe—land where cultivation was ancient and well understood. North America was a very different place, and even if Thomas Jefferson didn't know this before 1806, he sure should have suspected it when Lewis and Clark turned in their report on the land beyond the Missouri River. In his boosterism of the yeoman farmer, Jefferson was not the visionary he is sometimes cracked up to be. By the time of the

Homestead Act of 1862, even the well-watered farmland of New England and the slaveholding South was already wearing out.

Unlike Europe, the Great Plains had no long-established agrarian culture complete with management techniques learned over thousands of years of trial and error. While a few acres in Belgium could sustain a family, only a few select 160-acre plots could sustain a family in the tallgrass region of the Great Plains, and almost none could farther west where the grass varieties were shorter. As homesteading crept from the forty-inches-per-year rainfall belt along the eastern border of the Great Plains toward where rainfall seldom amounted to more than ten inches per year, the legal size of the homesteads eventually rose from the initial 160 acres to 640 acres. Still, the homesteaders were set up to fail, and about 40 percent of them did.

In addition to the 80 million acres granted to homesteaders, the U.S. government gave an additional 185 million acres to the largest industry of the day. In a scheme hatched while the Civil War was still raging in the east, the railroads were given not only rights-of-way to build lines to the fledgling communities scattered across the Great Plains and to the Pacific Ocean but also alternate sections within ten miles of that right-of-way in a checkerboard pattern, plus plots suitable for settlement at intervals of seven to ten miles. These town sites were shamelessly promoted to unsuspecting immigrants as oases and the future sites of important cities equivalent to Chicago, Saint Louis, or San Francisco. In truth, most settlers and railroad towns lasted no more than a few years. While the railroad companies claimed to be performing the public service of opening the West, their activities were, in fact, one of the great business scams of all time. The idea was to lay tracks ahead of the settlers pushing westward and control their activities for the benefit of the shareholders of the companies. The railroads deceptively advertised and sold to innocent settlers the land that had been given to them. They charged those settlers for transportation of themselves and their families and building material for their homes and barns. If the settlers managed to grow a cash crop on their meager holdings, the railroad overcharged them to carry it to eastern markets. Of course, the settlers seldom raised a substantial crop, and the communities seldom materialized. Many people moved on, some even poorer than they began. But before they moved on they gathered and burned the dried buffalo chips of the receding herds to heat their hovels during those hard Great Plains winters and gathered buffalo bones to sell in the east for fertilizer. A carload of buffalo bones was often the only shipment they ever made. The only mention of buffalo in the literature of the railroad companies was to advertise the opportunity to indiscriminately shoot them from their moving railroad cars, for a handsome fee.

Most of the railroad towns along the spur tracks were poor substitutes for the trade centers that the Indians had established and used for centuries. They withered, dried up, and blew away. But the main tracks, and the telegraph poles alongside them, stretched clear to the Pacific Ocean. The transcontinental tracks split the great buffalo herd into two nearly separate herds. It was unintentional, but, looking back and understanding that the concerted effort to exterminate the buffalo would soon follow, the railroads' actions look like the old tactic of divide and conquer. The southern herd would be gone twenty years after the first carload of immigrants crossed the Missouri. The northern herd would hold on, protected by their Indian brothers for another decade, but the tragic machine had been switched on, and it would continue to grind until the deed was done.

In the case of the destruction of the natural ecosystem of the Great Plains, the tragic machine was a brand of capitalism that was ruthless, ignorant, and blind. Steam and steel had been pressed into service by men with little knowledge of how the natural world works or any concept of restraint. Nineteenth-century American industrialists, particularly those involved in railroads, mining interests, and forestry, rushed to the Great Plains, where they could use their capital and connections in the U.S. Congress to exploit this new land. They had little regard for the settlers or the Indians and never gave a thought to the nonhuman inhabitants. The less sophisticated people of the Great Plains and the grasses that underpinned the ecosystem had all the stress they could handle in surviving the bitter winters and the desiccating droughts. This wild, nineteenth-century capitalism was overwhelming and impossible to withstand.

As early as 1870 a few newspaper and magazine writers were describing America's industrialists as robber barons, a term used to describe ancient European rulers who charged tolls for passage on roads traversing their land. The implication was that this so-called aristocracy was not only illegitimate but anathema in a republic. In August 1870 the *Atlantic* magazine claimed that "the old robber barons of the middle ages who plunder sword in hand . . . were more honest than this new aristocracy of swindling millionaires." The Great Plains and the buffalo were no match for such marauders, and they fell before their machines in due time. But not before putting up a fight.

One of the first to speak up was John Wesley Powell, most famous for his harrowing first decent of the Colorado River, but more important for his realistic appraisal of what was then known as the West. He was a born naturalist and conservationist. At a young age Powell explored the river systems of the Midwest, studied Greek and Latin, then joined the Union army as a private in the Civil War. At the Battle of Shiloh he lost an arm but returned to duty and rose to the level of brevet lieutenant colonel. He likely saw his first buffalo in 1869 when he renewed his childhood obsession with traveling rivers and, as a professor at Illinois Wesleyan University, organized an expedition to explore the West. Powell was a thoughtful man, and it would have been impossible for him to view the great herds and not realize that they were critical to the environment of the plains—and doomed.

Powell went on to government posts involving geology, hydrology, and ethnology. He used his position as the second director of the U.S. Geological Survey to argue for conservation and preservation. He argued for the commonsense strategy of defining new states to be admitted to the Union by river drainages instead of arbitrary political boundaries and famously stated that the arid West was not suitable for agriculture—both assertions that the buffalo he met in his travels could have confirmed.

Not all of Powell's theories and predictions turned out to be true, but his belief that the American West was prone to extended droughts and should not be farmed proved to be right when the Dust Bowl of the 1930s hit the Great Plains. But the railroads lobbied against Powell's thoughtful arguments in Congress. In typical industrialist fashion, they chose the "scientific" theory that served their purpose best. Horace Greeley and particularly a professor at Southern Illinois University named Cyrus Thomas championed a theory that advised people not to worry about rainfall on the Great Plains because "rain followed the plow." Thomas, who was also an entomologist and archeologist, believed that increased human population and cultivation would somehow increase rainfall. It was a completely crackpot idea but just the theory that the railroads needed to push their agenda in Congress. The robber barons applied their influence and more thoughtful voices, like John Wesley Powell's, were drowned out by the "Ca-ching!" of cash registers, and another nail was driven into the coffin of the Great Plains and through the heart of the buffalo.

CHAPTER THREE

Cleansing the Land

Killing the Buffalo on the Central and Southern Plains

Even before North America was severed from Asia the ancestors of modern buffalo were pursued by men. Buffalo might not have understood how dangerous humans would one day become, but they usually avoided the clumsy, low-tech men who occasionally ambushed them with clubs and spears. They did not yet have the mobility to hunt buffalo effectively. The famous "wild" horses of the American West were far in the future and never really wild. They were feral—domestic horses released or lost into the wild.

The animals that we know as horses are a product of Eurasian herding people who bred them from several subspecies that existed on the steppes of Europe. So, far from being the iconic indigenous equine of the Great Plains, the modern horse was a creation of Eurasian man. They did not rise out of the genetic goop of prehistoric America but from the holds of the Spanish galleons of Cortés and Coronado. When the Indians recovered from the shock of seeing them carrying soldiers bent on pillaging their civilizations, they must have begun dreaming of possessing horses of their own. By the time the Spanish reached buffalo country, clever Indians were stealing horses from the conquistadores and working out how they could be used to kill buffalo. That was around 1600. By the late 1700s the horse had spread to nearly all the Great Plains tribes and those tribes had emerged from the shadows of the river bottoms and onto the open plains. Suddenly they were mobile and, to the young men of the tribe, the idea of hoeing beans and squash lost its appeal. The grandmothers must have thrown up their hands. How you going to keep them down on the farm once they've seen a horse?

The buffalo could no longer amble away from a group of would-be hunters. Now, to escape the hunters, they would have to learn to run. Those first semiorganized buffalo hunts from horseback must have been a sight. Up out of the river bottom come a half dozen teenage boys clinging to the backs of semi-wild horses they have stolen from a Spanish camp; no saddle, not much for reins, a clumsy spear or a club in one hand, the other hand twisted into the mane. They ride straight toward the small buffalo herd that stands staring at this strange new sight. The horses gain speed and the boys bounce and slide left and right. One accidently pokes his mount with the spear and the horse goes into a bucking spree, tossing the boy off but continuing, riderless, into the herd. The buffalo are not sure what to think. This first attack does not look dangerous but one of the boys, mounted on a stout gray horse with a magpie feather braded into its tail, has a certain knack and is able to flatten himself over his horse's back. He leans forward and puts his cheek against the gray's muscular neck. A yearling cow raises her head and stares in amazement. What could this be? She nearly stands on tiptoes and turns slightly as the boy and the gray blend together and the speed increases even more. Behind them, the other boys are in disarray. Two more have come off their horses and a couple are hanging on the side with both hands gripping the mane. The horses dodge prairie dog holes and another rider flies, hits, and bounces in a cloud of dust. But the gray keeps coming. The boy on the gray has thought this through. In the exhausted, sore-muscle nights of the last weeks when he was learning to ride the stolen gray he dreamed about this very moment. He raises the spear tip as he passes the young cow.

The impact nearly knocks him from the gray's back, but his legs tighten and he stays on and pulls the horse to a jarring stop. The herd has begun to run and now all the other riders are either dismounted or disarmed. Boys are trying to catch their horses or looking for the clubs and spears that dropped during their charge. But one spear is easy to find. It stands upright, with a magpie feather tied to the shaft and flapping in the prairie breeze. The magpie feather is exactly like the one tied to tail of the gray horse who stands stomping and trying to sidestep under the boy. Ordinarily he would be laughing at his friends but he can't take his eyes away from that spear shaft and the magpie feather. His eyes are wide and his jaw is slack. At the other end of the spear is a brown mound that he knows is the young buffalo. Her feet windmill and kick up dust as she dies. The boy lays a hand on the gray's shoulder to calm him and the other boys stop to look. Everyone—the boys, the gray horse, and the rest of the buffalo herd that now stands looking back from the top of the next hill—realize that nothing will ever be the same.

Some tribes completely severed their ties to the farm fields along the rivers and set out across the plains—powered by horses. They followed the buffalo to places that they had never been before. With horses to carry their belongings they developed buffalo-hide tents, much too heavy to carry on a human's back or to be dragged by dogs. They changed their diet to mostly meat. They learned to glean everything they needed from the buffalo that they could now kill at almost any time. Now they could bring their babies and old people with them. Life became immeasurably easier, and they were thankful. They built a culture around buffalo and horses, and by the time the Euro-Americans made their way to the Great Plains, it appeared that the Plains Indians had always lived this way.

Horses spread to the entire Great Plains, though early on they were much more prevalent in the south, where the Spanish first introduced them. The relatively mild climate allowed horses to thrive in summer and winter, and the Indians' herds grew to enormous size. The Pueblo Indians revolted against the Spanish in 1680 and confiscated thousands of cattle, sheep, and horses. They integrated the cattle and particularly the sheep into their agrarian culture and initiated what would become a tremendous intertribal trade in horses. They traded horses to the Comanches and Navajos and the horse moved northward, using established trade routes and stimulating more routes until by 1770 horses were ubiquitous from old Mexico to the prairies of British America. Stimulated by the unparalleled quality of the grasslands, horse numbers exploded. On the southern plains the horse herds eventually numbered in the tens of thousands and, early on, began to compete with the buffalo for forage, even as they aided the Indians in killing the buffalo with growing ease.

Intertribal trading had existed for centuries but had been limited. With the European invasion came trade not only in horses but also in goods from the white man's culture. Because horses supplied a much better means of transportation to the ports along the larger rivers, there was a general increase in trade, including in buffalo robes and meat that had theretofore been too heavy to move easily. Horses were so coveted by northern tribes that they began raiding other tribes and attacking white settlers for their horses. Tensions and warfare over hunting grounds increased, as did the capture of women, who were forced to process buffalo hides or were traded directly to southern tribes in exchange for more horses.

The acquisition of horses was a technological change that must have seemed like a tremendous leap forward. It gave the tribes mobility and access to wealth that they had never known. But that wealth was dependent on buffalo, and as the tribes began to specialize in year-round buffalo hunting, they abandoned their traditional, more diverse, economy of mixing limited pedestrian buffalo hunting, farming, and gathering. The safety net of diversity crumbled and with it a centuries-old sustainable culture. From mostly stationary cultures, the tribes became nomads with a decentralized social structure and unwittingly rushed into a life dependent on a single resource, buffalo. They chose specialization over diversity—the tragic flaw of the human experience on the Great Plains.

Trade in buffalo hides and meat for farm products like corn, squash, and tobacco had been a fixture on the Great Plains for hundreds of years, but now it expanded beyond the still-sedentary river tribes to the invading Europeans. The wonders of Europe, and increasingly, industrial eastern America, filtered into trading posts along the western rivers. Buffalo tongues and dried buffalo meat began to be shipped to eastern cities by the ton, and Indians were the principal procurers. Buffalo robes came into fashion as winter throws to cover the laps of passengers in eastern buggies. With the advent of this new means to wealth, avarice and greed bloomed in the Indian mind and drove them to atrocities against their brothers. Tribal warfare increased across the plains, and a further breakdown of their traditional social structure followed.

In one case a small group of Lakota Sioux killed about fifteen hundred buffalo in a single day and took only their tongues to trade at a fort on the Missouri. Newfound horse mobility had allowed Indian society to fracture into small, independent groups.

With a growing market for buffalo robes came a need to

expand their traditions of polygamy to meet the need for female hide processors. The female slave trade increased dramatically to supply even more hide processors, and so more hides for trade and more wealth for the men of the group, who had long since given up their farmer's hoe and hide-scrapping tools for their horse herds, hunting spears, new rifles, and a freewheeling life.

Even the relatively small trade in buffalo meat and hides before the 1830s must have felt like a betrayal to the buffalo. The Indians had always believed in a special relationship between themselves and the buffalo. In a spiritual, metaphoric sense there was a sort of deal between the Indian nation and the buffalo nation. The buffalo nation would sacrifice a few of its citizens to the Indian nation and so supply that nation with all it needed to survive—food, shelter, and warmth in the wintertime. All the Indian nation had to do was to respect the buffalo nation as an equal. That respect began to crumble when Indians began to commoditize their brothers, the buffalo. The Indians were never supposed to glean a surplus from the buffalo, but in the first half of the nineteenth century, in addition to tongues and dried flesh, bundles of buffalo hides began disappearing into the holds of riverboats heading for Boston, New York, and Philadelphia. A sacred trust was under strain. After the Civil War the trust would dissolve in the onslaught of white war veterans, settlers, and entrepreneurs who would more completely unravel the Great Plains fabric that the buffalo had held together for thousands of years. When European tanneries sent word that they had mastered the techniques required to turn dry buffalo hides into supple, strong leather, a new generation of hide hunters made their way to the Great Plains.

North America had been feeling the tentacles of the Old World economy crawling up its river systems for two hundred years, but with the opening of international trade in buffalo hides the grip began to tighten. The remnants of the American beaver trappers, and many others, began to gear up to supply the world with buffalo hides.

By 1830 John Jacob Astor's company, the American Fur Company, had monopolized the fur trade in North America and, largely by siphoning off wealth from the Great Plains, Astor had become the country's first multimillionaire. He created the first trust and set his descendants up to remain one of the richest families in America for generations to come. When the beaver business began to crash Astor cashed out, but his company began to focus on moving buffalo hides through the system of trading posts Astor had established on the Great Plains.

Ecology and economy have always been inseparable and, unfortunately, ecology often suffers with the enhancement of economy. That was certainly the case with the slaughter of millions of buffalo in the last half of the nineteenth century. It began slowly, with Indians encouraged to do the dirty work, but as they began to realize that their brothers and sisters were not an inexhaustible resource and that all that killing was only speeding the takeover of their land by settlers, they began to push back. Hostilities flared up and the trappers, turned buffalo hunters, were not safe unless they came with enough force to discourage the Indians from stealing their horses and killing them in their sleep.

During the Civil War the United States' attention was diverted and, along with the Treaty of Fort Laramie in 1851 that gave settlers right of passage through the buffalo-hunting grounds of the northern tribes, that led to a lull in hostilities. But on the central plains, in the heart of the buffalo range of western Kansas, eastern Colorado, and southern Nebraska, the battles between Cheyenne, Lakota, and Arapaho warriors and American miners and settlers became brutal. Indian encampments along rivers that would soon be famous for the slaughter of great quantities of buffalo were attacked mercilessly. In

Kansas and Nebraska, no Indian along the Arkansas, the Smoke Hill, the Republican, and the Platte Rivers was safe. At Sand Creek in present-day Colorado, where Southern Cheyenne warriors had gone buffalo hunting and left only a skeleton crew to protect the women and children, seven hundred drunken militiamen slaughtered, scalped, and mutilated 133 peaceful souls who were flying over their camp both an American flag and a white flag of surrender. Of the 105 women and children who were killed, most were obscenely dismembered. An aged leader of the Cheyennes, White Antelope, had his ears, nose, and testicles cut off by a militiaman. His scrotum was made into a tobacco pouch.

Though most of the massacred Indians who died on the southern plains died in their camps, many were hunted down like vermin and their bodies were spread across the prairie where their people had hunted buffalo for hundreds of years. Certainly, as the herds moved across those prairies during the early and mid-1860s, they came across mangled bodies of the people who had once been their respectful relations. It runs counter to all modern thinking about the cognition of animals, but I suspect that when a buffalo came across the deteriorating remains of a Cheyenne, Arapaho, or Kiowa, a precise and meaningful moan rumbled in his throat that called his herd mates to the sight. I imagine them standing shoulder to shoulder, switching their tails, swinging their wooly heads, and in that way, mourning the passing of their brothers and their fall from grace.

When the Civil War ended, great American military heroes like Generals Sherman, Sheridan, and Custer were put in charge of dozens of forts constructed as a deterrent to Indian raids. During the Civil War these generals had learned that destruction of the enemy's food source was one of the surest ways to win a war. Sherman had become famous for his scorched earth policy during his devastating "March to the Sea" through Georgia. He not only burned the plantations, railroads, and armament facilities he came to, but also the crops in the fields. He destroyed the Rebel commissary and surrender followed soon after. The same strategy was adopted by the Americans on the Great Plains except, in the case of the Indians, the commissary was the buffalo. The generals began to kill buffalo every chance they got, but it soon became clear that even regiments of soldiers would be insufficient to kill enough buffalo to starve the Indians. Instead, as a matter of course, the army sponsored and outfitted civilian hide hunters to kill the buffalo. They also supplied ammunition, shelter, and protection from Indians. In this way, the southern and central plains were nearly cleared of buffalo. Almost all of the millions of buffalo killed in this way were stripped naked of the hides and left to rot on the plains. The strategy worked. By the late 1870s the Indians of the southern plains were reduced to paupers.

The industries of the world were howling for more buffalo hides to make leather belting to move power from one rotating shaft of a machine to another shaft and so to allow industry to march forward. In the late 1860s and 1870s smaller groups of men—many of them Civil War veterans—came to the killing fields of Kansas, Oklahoma, and the panhandle of Texas. For a minimal investment they could purchase a couple wagons, a few cans of beans, a powerful rifle, and enough powder and shot to kill a thousand buffalo. The independent hide hunters mutilated the buffalo like the militias mutilated the Indians. In most cases they took only the hides, ten, twenty, a hundred a day.

The main hunter would usually do the shooting, starting early on beautiful prairie mornings so that the skinners could strip the hides and stake them out to dry before dark, when the wolves would move in to claim their share. In the 1870s the wolf population on the southern plains soared. They could not begin to eat the slaughtered buffalo that covered the prairie. Before the hide hunters came, wolves had to work for their meals, mostly old bulls, cows, or calves caught too far from their mothers. Now there were whole herds of starving, orphaned calves. But even pulling those babies down was too much work, compared to feasting on the naked, bloating bodies of their mothers strewn to the horizon. Those years were heaven for wolves and other predators. Their coats were luxuriant and shiny, their litters large. Winter could not kill them, and the hunters were so intent on killing more buffalo that at first they ignored the wolves. Wolves shadowed the hunters in packs of hundreds, and there were plenty of hunters.

By the early 1870s an estimated two thousand commercial hide hunters were working out of Dodge City, Kansas, whose population at the time was about five hundred. Every other railhead had similar numbers of hunters who shipped the results of their hunts back east. Though hides were the main prize, some buffalo tongues and select meats were shipped east in the cool seasons. But the vast majority of the buffalo was left on the prairie, even when rail transport was close to the killing grounds.

Railroads had opened the southern and central buffalo grounds to Americans, and they continued to niggle into areas where buffalo were finding temporary safe havens. One of America's most famous western icons, Buffalo Bill, made his name by supplying meat for construction crews of the Kansas Pacific Railroad Company. He killed 4,280 buffalo in eighteen months and bragged about it for the rest of his long life. Other men probably killed more buffalo on the Kansas Plains than Cody—millions died there between 1870 and 1875—but Cody also orchestrated the deaths of many more at the hands of rich or royal hunters that he guided. From killing to guiding and eventually to exhibiting them in his Wild West shows, Cody was the master exploiter of the buffalo.

When the giant herds of western Kansas and eastern Colorado were almost gone the hunters moved to the panhandle of Texas, where the buffalo were still common and the railroad was accessible to carry their hides to market. They skirted Indian Territory, the land south of the Arkansas River that had been set aside for Comanches, Cheyennes, Arapahoes, and Kiowas, not out of respect for the Medicine Lodge Treaty of 1867 that supposedly secured the land for the tribes but because they were afraid of losing their scalps. But it didn't take long for the hide hunters to break the treaty and enter Indian Territory, where there were still huge herds. When that happened, the merchants of Dodge City, realizing that their business was dying, followed the hide hunters into Indian Territory and, at the site of Adobe Walls, constructed an illegal trading town in 1874. A month after it was established five hundred Indians attacked the town. They killed three white men, but thirteen Indians died defending their buffalo.

Though Adobe Walls was soon abandoned, the incident set Cheyenne, Kiowa, and Arapahoe warriors on the warpath across the region. They raided not only in Indian Territory but north of the Arkansas River and deeper into Texas. Settlers, railroaders, and hide hunters were attacked and killed. Some of the hide hunters who escaped the uprising fled the southern plains and migrated northward to ply their trade on the northern herds. But a precedent had been set. The northern tribes would not be passive. They would fight for their buffalo.

CHAPTER FOUR

The Empty Land

The Slaughter Moves North

In the mid-1800s Mormons began to move from all over the eastern part of America, and even Europe, toward the Great Salt Lake in what became Utah Territory. The Treaty of Guadalupe Hidalgo had awarded the territory to America after the Mexican-American War. The Mormons were early travelers along the Platte River where the transcontinental railroad would soon be built. The disturbance caused by commerce along that route had already begun to split the buffalo herd into a northern herd and a southern herd, but the Mormons saw plenty of buffalo on their trek west. In fact, many of them lived off buffalo meat for weeks at a time.

Imagine a group of young bull buffalo strung out on a ridge-top on the north side of the Platte River. They are silhouetted against a powder-blue prairie sky and appear black to the Mormons walking alongside a wagon train winding for a mile beside the river. These are poor people; some are pushing carts or carrying their possessions on their backs. Their most valued possession is the herd of cattle strung out behind the wagon train, with women and children at the very end driving old and weak animals forward. The wagons are pulled by oxen, whipped by men, because there are few horses. The buffalo have never seen cattle or Mormons. In the buffalo's experience, the only thing the wagon train resembles is a caterpillar, seen up close in a prairie dog town where the buffalo have stopped to roll in the dust. In fact, these people are refugees from the turbulent eastern United States. They are exiles: a combative breed from a bellicose nation, intent on conquest and laboring under the belief that they are God's chosen people.

In the autumn of 1854, near the boundary of what is now Nebraska and Wyoming, buffalo were scarce because wagon-loads of Mormons had frightened them out of the Platte River Valley. A group of Lakota people, camped near Fort Laramie, were waiting for the rations of food they had been promised in the Treaty of 1851. The promised rations were already many days late, and the younger warriors were growing impatient. A Miniconjou warrior named High Forehead had a family to feed and he was searching for buffalo when he came across a Mormon cow straggling far behind the wagon train and killed it for food.

The Mormons were enraged and rode into Fort Laramie to demand that High Forehead pay for the cow and be punished. High Forehead had no money and took refuge in the camp of Conquering Bear, who was a leader of the Brule Band of Lakotas. When the senior officer at the fort asked Conquering Bear to give up High Forehead, he said that High Forehead was a Miniconjou and that he could not give up a member of another band. He refused the request in no uncertain terms. Second Lieutenant John Grattan, a very recent West Point graduate, was offended by Conquering Bear's attitude and took it upon himself to avenge the loss of the Mormon cow. Fueled by ignorance and righteous indignation, he led twenty-nine other men into Conquering Bear's camp.

There was a heated discussion, and the fireworks began when an anxious solder under Grattan's command shot Conquering Bear in the back. Cold-blooded murder. The Lakota warriors, led by the up-and-coming war chiefs Red Cloud and Spotted Tail, quickly flanked Grattan and showed him a few techniques he hadn't learned at West Point. Without losing another man, Red Cloud and Spotted Tail killed Grattan and all of his men. This would not be the last the Americans heard of Red Cloud and Spotted Tail. The war for the northern buffalo-hunting grounds had begun, and Red Cloud and Spotted Tail would lead their bands of Oglala and Miniconjou Sioux in continuous brutal battles, through desperate winters, and in specious negotiations for the next thirty-five years.

The buffalo on the southern plains, below the Platte River, had been hunted until they were reduced to fugitives, constantly harassed and slaughtered with no mercy. At the end of the 1870s small groups might still be sighted in the panhandle of Texas, and dozens of self-appointed vigilantes would rally to track them down. Handfuls of buffalo cows with their calves were surrounded by cowboys who were moving into Kansas and eastern Colorado. The cows would be shot and the calves roped and dragged back to corrals at ranch headquarters as curiosities. Most of the calves died of a combination of poor feed and lack of a functioning herd structure. Those who understood buffalo said they died of broken hearts and loneliness.

With the herds reduced to stragglers, the hide hunters moved north, up the Missouri River along the eastern flank of the remaining buffalo territory that was then still protected by the Lakota, Blackfeet, Cheyenne, and Crow Nations, who had not given up their land. The hide hunters based their operations at military forts built along the Missouri and functioning as trading posts and makeshift communities, poised like vultures next to the Great Sioux Reservation that would eventually be opened up for Anglo homesteading. On much of that tremendous piece of land, the buffalo hardly knew that they were under siege, but the noose was tightening. More American forts were being built along the Missouri River, the Platte River was awash with pioneers, miners had infiltrated the western mountains, and Washington and Oregon were filling up with farmers and timbermen.

But for now on the northern buffalo range, in midsummer, the calves' coats still began to turn from golden yellow to the brown coloration of the rest of the herd. In June they lay curled in the drying grass or played with their friends as the adults began to breed. On the northern plains things continued much as they had done for thousands of years. The bulls roared and bellowed. Their goatees, pantaloons, and headdresses grew to breeding length. They urinated in dusty wallows and rolled. Dust rose from their wallowing, from their shaking, and from their movement across the prairie.

In July and August the behavior of the bulls turned to haughty belligerence. They confronted, stalked, and stood ceremonially eyeballing other bulls. They pushed and shoved but they seldom came to blows. Actual combat was not the best use of the energy they had stored throughout the green-grass days of spring. In late summer almost all activity was directed toward breeding—passing genes on to the next generation.

In those undisturbed pastures of the northern Great Plains in the mid-nineteenth century it was still possible to carry on life as it had been before hide hunters flooded the land, before the horse came to the continent, and before traders began offering the buffalo's brothers and sisters unimaginable luxuries for betraying them. On the northern Great Plains during the slaughter on the southern plains, life was still good. The cows walked nonchalantly through the herds that had gathered to enormous size. They flicked their tails and the bulls followed them until one bull, by force of his bellowing, or size, or some unknowable magnetism, moved up beside a cow and became her tender. He positioned himself between her and the rest of the herd, shielding her from the sight of other bulls who hovered at the edge of this tête-à-tête. Occasionally she would take a notion to drive him wild by running through the herd and showing herself to the other bachelors. Her tender would stay right with her, fumbling along behind, trying to stay beside her, awkwardly striving to remain the object of her affection. The lesser bachelors followed in the crazy chase and the dust rose in billows. Seen from above, a big herd would have looked like a sea of writhing brown with golden highlights. Mixed in the sea would be contrails of coquettish buffalo cows with two-thousand-pound, blustering suitors thundering in their wake.

Finally, toward the end of August the wild courtships ended. Eighty-five percent of all the adult cows were bred, and all energies turned to the serious business of laying on winter fat to make it through the trial of a Great Plains winter. Since late March the sun had been transferring its energy to the grass. Now the buffalo harvested that energy. Everyone grew butterball fat and the great herds dispersed into smaller groups. The bulls stopped their grumbling, stomping, and shaking of their wooly heads at each other. They wandered off in small bachelor groups to recuperate and enjoy the cool nights and warm autumn afternoons dozing on grassy hillsides.

When the Americans were at war among themselves and even with the slaughter on the southern plains about to reach epic proportions, resistance from the northern tribes suppressed the hide trade along the upper Missouri. Occasionally the northern Indians came and took their subsistence from the scattered herds. They guarded their hunting grounds and, where they were able, kept strangers out.

In the north, winter was another factor that kept the hide hunters away. Every year it came on in the usual, unpredictable way; some years the water was not yet frozen when the shortest day came and sometimes it was so cold and dark that the Indians huddled in their teepees for days at a time. But the buffalo stood on the hilltops where the snow was most likely to blow away and reveal the winter grass that, on the northern plains, retained its nutrition under any conditions. Even if the snow lay two feet deep the buffalo swung their heads and plowed down to graze, seemingly unfazed. The wind and wolves howled and took their share like the Indians, but the strongest buffalo survived and thrived. In those halcyon days before the hide hunters moved north, times were sweet. Millions of buffalo lived to see the green grass emerge from the snowdrifts, and the cycle began again.

The calves were born beginning at the end of March. A buffalo cow felt the movement inside of her and knew when to break away from the small family group that she had spent the winter with. Often the group consisted of her mother, aunts, and sisters. A few yearly bulls might have attached themselves to the group, but the old bulls were nowhere to be seen and offered little protection from the wolves that gathered by the dozens. A cow would not go far from the herd but far enough to be in danger, and much depended on how quickly she could give birth to her calf, get it on its feet, and return to the herd. Wolves killed a percentage of the calves, but the cows were aggressive and belligerent protectors of their young. For most of a day the cow moved uncomfortably from one position to another. She fidgeted, laid down, got up, laid down again, rolled, until finally her water broke and the front feet of the calf appeared. By then she was on her side and the contractions came quickly. All the time, wolves were moving closer. But as soon as the calf was born, the cow was on her feet licking her offspring clean and staring down the wolves who circled her and her baby.

As with everything about a buffalo, the horns evolved to help carry the genes of each particular buffalo on to the next generation. The horns of bulls are wide and very thick at the base. They are not sharp but massive enough to intimidate rivals. If the threat does not work to ensure the bull's right to breed, the horns are stout enough to absorb earth-shaking collisions with the competition. They can be lethal but nothing like the tight, rapier-like horns of the cows. Their horns are thin at the base and curve upward with a gut-tearing twist. The horns of buffalo cows evolved to fight wolves, and their genes enable them to accelerate in an instant. They are very athletic and could chase a wolf at top speed, then turn and be back to the calf in time to flip a second wolf ten feet into the air. Their effectiveness in this kind of battle is the calf's edge to survival. If its mother could keep the wolves away until the calf was up on its feet, there was a good chance they would make it back to the herd, where aunts and grandmothers could join in the fight.

By the end of June, most of the calves were on the ground. Calves are golden and when scattered across a valley or sunlit hillside they look much like a clump of last year's bluestem grass. They sleep curled up and perfectly still, but when they wake up they run and play at top speed. They are tiny compared to the adults and from a distance, a dozen newborn buffalo calves are reminiscent of bumble bees moving frenetically from flower to flower. By July and August, when the small groups joined again to form huge herds and the bulls wandered back with roars and foot stomping, the calves were beginning to lose their golden coats and stand goofy and awkward as teenagers at a wedding. During the Civil War the northern plains had a respite from the chaos of conquest. It was a time when the hardships and dangers for the buffalo were only ordinary. The buffalo that lived at that time and in that place were the last to enjoy true freedom. They were the last to live in an untrammeled land and to be real buffalo—unfettered and mythic.

It had not taken hide hunters long to exterminate the buffalo herds of the central and southern plains, but on the northern plains the buffalo herd was still healthy and Indians were rich, proud, and defiant. Gold was discovered in Montana in the late 1850s, and by 1863 John Bozeman had blazed a trail from Fort Laramie on the Oregon Trail to the new goldfields in the western mountains. People and freight began to move up that trail and through the Powder River Country. That might have been all right with some Indians, but not Red Cloud, one of the principals in the battle that avenged the murder of Conquering Bear after the Mormon cow incident; he had matured into a pugnacious Lakota leader who liked to spend his time hunting buffalo on the plains just east of the Big Horn Mountains, where the Powder River flowed. The Powder River Country was a refuge not only for the buffalo nation but also for Cheyennes, Arapahoes, and several bands of Lakotas—including Red Cloud's Oglalas.

Thousands of miners and settlers heading for the west used the Bozeman Trail and, of course, helped themselves to all the buffalo they could shoot. Red Cloud could tolerate people passing through his country, but slaughtering buffalo, and again leaving most of them to rot, pushed him to open warfare. For two years he and other headmen led a guerrilla war in defense of their buffalo-hunting grounds. In one notable battle they were very successful, killing an entire command of eighty-two men. In that battle, called the Fetterman Fight, a young Lakota leader rose to prominence thanks to a decoying technique for which he would become famous. That leader was Crazy Horse. The allied Indian force put up such a fight that the forts along the Bozeman Trail, built by the U.S. government to protect settlers and miners, were abandoned. Red Cloud refused to negotiate for peace until all the forts were burned to the ground. Even then he was three months late to the treaty council—he would not cut short his annual buffalo hunt for the convenience of a few generals and commissioners from Washington DC.

The 1868 Treaty of Fort Laramie, which ended Red Cloud's War, forbade any white man (except U.S. government officials) from setting foot on the Great Sioux Reservation that included the Black Hills and all of the Dakotas west of the Missouri River. It also set aside all the land between the Black Hills and the Rocky Mountains as an unceded Indian territory. The Great Sioux Reservation was meant to be a sanctuary for the Indians and the Powder River Country a sanctuary for the buffalo. But, of course, it didn't last.

In August 1874 George Armstrong Custer, a brash young Civil War hero who had made a name as an Indian fighter on the southern plains, led a legally questionable expedition into the Black Hills in what would become South Dakota. The group discovered gold, and civilian miners soon rushed to the spot. But the Black Hills were in the heart of Indian Territory—specifically out of bounds for whites. In addition to this incursion, plans were being made to push the Northern Pacific Railroad through the home of the northern buffalo herd. Red Cloud had retired to the reservation, but most of the Northern Cheyenne and Lakota bands headed now by Sitting Bull and Crazy Horse had retreated to the unceded country, where they could eat buffalo instead of the stringy cattle that were then being delivered to the reservation towns from the southern plains.

There was great pressure for these bands to leave the unceded buffalo sanctuary and join the Indians who had accepted life on the reservations, where buffalo were nearly extinct. Cheyenne, Lakota, and Arapaho warriors tried to keep the miners out of the Black Hills, and they killed a few in minor skirmishes. The United States reacted to these killings with indignation and ordered the Indians to leave the unceded land and move to the reservations by January 31, 1876.

By then army forts nearly surrounded the Indians and most

of the buffalo—from Fort Laramie in what is now Wyoming, along the southern border of South Dakota, up the Missouri River to Bismarck, North Dakota, and along the Yellowstone River to Bozeman, Montana. From those forts the Americans sent expeditions into Indian Territory. After the deadline for the Indians to be on the reservations came and went, the army moved in force on February 8, 1876.

That spring three fingers of a pincher began to close on the free Indians who were still in their winter buffalo camps in the Powder River Country. General George Crook came from Fort Fetterman to the south. Colonel John Gibbon marched from Fort Ellis to the west. General Alfred Terry left Fort Abraham Lincoln far to the east on the Missouri. Commanding the seven hundred men of Terry's Seventh Calvary was Lieutenant Colonel Custer. The pincher closed on its prey, but the prey bit back.

On June 25, 1876, Custer found the camp of Two Moons, Gall, Lame White Man, Sitting Bull, and Crazy Horse on the Little Bighorn River. It was the largest Indian camp that any of Custer's scouts had ever seen, probably three warriors to each of Custer's nearly 647 men. The warriors, along with their women and children, were camped in the Powder River Country, surrounded by their brothers and sisters—the buffalo. The camp was just waking up when the blue-coated horsemen snaked down into the river bottom. That is when the soldiers saw the extent of the camp. It stretched for two miles, and no one was running away. In fact, the Indian leaders rallied their men and soon Custer himself was on the run. The Indians killed and mutilated 268 men and took sadistic revenge on the body of Custer for his transgressions—most specifically his incursion into the Black Hills.

For the next year the Indians of the northern Great Plains were hunted like their four-legged brothers and sisters had been hunted on the southern plains. All through that winter soldiers tracked the Sioux, Cheyennes, and other tribes and attacked their villages and camps, chasing the old people, women, and children into the wind and snow. There was no time for hunting buffalo, and the fugitives grew lean and weak with hunger. Battered groups wandered onto the reservations to be disarmed, dismounted, enrolled, and incarcerated on ever-shrinking islands of land. The last to come in was Crazy Horse. In the spring of the year after the killing of Custer, Crazy Horse and his gallant, freedom- and buffalo-loving band of 889 men, women, and children straggled out of the Powder River Country.

Like the buffalo, Indians had come up against a force more powerful than the thunderstorms that sweep the prairie every summer, stronger than flooding rivers, more formidable than subzero winds and drifting snow. U.S. policy toward Native Americans bounced between trying to assimilate the tribes into white culture and trying to exterminate them, but certainly the U.S. military, headed by then-president and Civil War hero Ulysses S. Grant, supported by close Civil War associates like William Sherman and Philip Sheridan, regarded Indians as an impediment to the "progress" of America. Their eradication, though perhaps repugnant in some ways, was considered inevitable and necessary.

In a letter to President Grant, Sherman said, "We must act with vindictive eagerness against the Sioux, even to their extermination, men, women and children." A few years earlier Sheridan had used the same language when speaking of the work of the hide hunters on the southern plains. "Let them kill, skin, and sell until the buffalo is exterminated." During the Civil War, Sherman and Sheridan had perfected a battle strategy they called "hard war," destroying all supplies and infrastructure, a strategy that contributed greatly to ending the Civil War. Demented as it was, equating the supplies and crops of Confederates to the buffalo of the Indians made some sense. After all, buffalo were everything to the entire ecosystem of the Great Plains, including Plains Indians. In the minds of American soldiers—and indeed in the minds of the Indians themselves—the buffalo, the Indian, and the land itself blurred into one thing.

The last gasp of free, equestrian, Great Plains Indians and the free buffalo nation took place about eight miles south of my house in December 1890. From where I sit in my writing chair, I can look out the window and see a long, flat butte rising out of the hazy distance, across the northwestern corner of the Pine Ridge Reservation. The beginning of the end occurred the year before, when the Lakotas heard about a religious man from the Paiute Tribe living in western Nevada. His name was Wovoka, and he claimed to have had a vision that the old people who had died, and the buffalo that had once sustained them, still lived and that they would come back to earth if the people prayed and danced in a certain way. All the evil that the white men had done would be reversed, and life would return to how it was before the Europeans appeared. Central to the appeal of the Ghost Dance was the belief that the buffalo would return.

Some say that Wovoka was claiming to be the resurrected Christ, and even though there is no Christ in native religion the possibility of the rebirth of loved ones, the buffalo, and the entire culture spread across the country. The Ghost Dance ignited the imaginations of many Indians, but especially people of the northern Great Plains. In fact, Wovoka was from a notoriously passive tribe who were preyed upon by Spaniards, Mexicans, and a host of other Indians. The Paiutes were known as an easy mark for marauders who captured their people—especially children and young women—and sold them into the slave trade. No one seemed to care that Wovoka was a member of a tribe that had never embraced the use of the horse and lived far beyond the range of the buffalo. The fact that Wovoka, from childhood to the age of about thirty, was employed and lived with an extremely fundamentalist Christian rancher seems never to have been taken into consideration. The idea of an Indian messiah who could deliver them from torment was too powerful to resist for the Lakota people, who had, by the end of the nineteenth century, been locked in mortal combat with the white invaders for forty years. Wovoka's vision found an ardent following in the Lakota bands who had been driven onto reservations after losing so many of their numbers, and nearly all of their brothers and sisters—the buffalo.

Wovoka was a pacifist, but the Lakotas added retribution and violence to his vision. In the eyes of the Lakota people, not only would the old people and the buffalo return, the whites would be driven back into the sea. The clock would be turned back to precontact days, as if contact had never happened. The Lakotas also added a costume and twist to the dances that were beginning to erupt on the reservations of the northern plains. They would wear Ghost Shirts—leather or cloth shirts decorated with images of deceased relatives, including the buffalo. The shirts would increase the potency of their prayers, and if the whites resisted and began shooting, the shirts would protect them from the bullets.

Sitting Bull was a leader of the Ghost Dance on his reservation along the North Dakota–South Dakota border. When he was shot and killed by Indian police, his followers fled from the Standing Rock Reservation and headed for the Pine Ridge Reservation. They picked up a Lakota leader named Big Foot on their way through the Cheyenne River Reservation and, though he was old and sick, Big Foot led them through the Badlands, toward the Ghost Dancers on Pine Ridge. But they only made it as far as Wounded Knee Creek, where they were surrounded by elements of what was left of Custer's Seventh Calvary. The Indians were held hostage in a winter camp, with four rapid-fire Hotchkiss guns pointing down on them, until the next morning, when the soldiers began to disarm them. It is not completely clear what happened, but the results are undisputable. The Hotchkiss guns fired, and the camp of 230 men and 120 women and children were caught in a cross fire. The initial attack did great damage to both the Indians and the soldiers, who came under friendly fire from their overzealous comrades. After the Hotchkiss guns fell silent, the soldiers tracked down and killed many of the Indians who had survived the shooting and had scattered into the hills. In the final tally of Indian casualties, there were 250 dead and 50 wounded. The army sustained 25 dead and 39 wounded.

Both Dee Brown, in *Bury My Heart at Wounded Knee*, and Black Elk, in *Black Elk Speaks*, describe the Wounded Knee massacre as the end of the Great Plains buffalo culture, but there was another short chapter. After the massacre, the Ghost Dancers fled to the same long, flat butte I can see from my window. They were terrified that the soldiers would follow and kill them, as they had killed the people at Wounded Knee, and dug in at the top of the nearly impregnable butte. Eventually they were talked down by a compassionate army officer, but they danced for days before they gave up the dream of the buffalo returning. We call the butte Stronghold Table, and for 120 years it loomed over a prairie devoid of buffalo. But now, on the grassland between our ranch house and Stronghold there are a few hundred buffalo. It is the pitifully small herd that my family and I watch over. These buffalo are only symbols of what used to be, but still—a few have returned. Sometimes at night, if the wind is out of the south and I hold my head just right, I believe I can hear Ghost Dance drums moving through swaying grass.

3. Bison grazed near Lake Jessie (Griggs County ND) when this was "Indian Country." John Mix Stanley made this engraving, *Herd of Bison near Lake Jesse*, when he traveled through northern Dakota Territory with the Northern Pacific Railroad survey crew in the 1860s. Travelers often remarked on the immense herds of bison they encountered on the Great Plains. Library of Congress, Prints and Photographs Division, LC-DIG-ppmsca-31596.

4. *Hunting the Buffaloe*, John T. Bowen, lithographer, ca. 1837. Library of Congress, Prints and Photographs Division, LC-DIG-pga-07508.

5. The Far West: Shooting buffalo on the line of the Kansas-Pacific Railroad, 1871. Library of Congress, Prints and Photographs Division, LC-USZ62–133890.

6. Soldiers pose with bison heads captured from poacher Ed Howell. When Howell returned to the park that year, he was the first person arrested and punished under the National Park Protection Act, passed in 1894. National Park Service, Department of the Interior.

7. *Slaughtered for the Hide, Harper's Weekly,* 1874. Library of Congress, Prints and Photographs Division, LC-USZ62–55602.

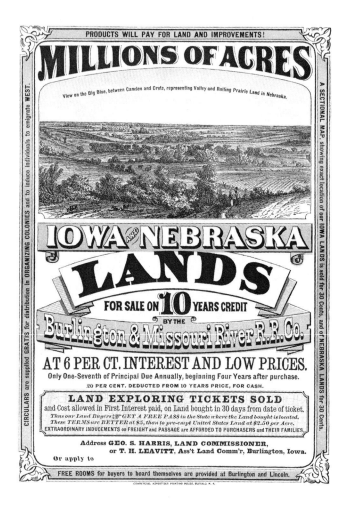

8. "Millions of acres of Iowa and Nebraska lands for sale on 10 years credit by the Burlington & Missouri River R. R. Co. at 6 per ct. interest and low prices." Buffalo NY, Commercial Advertiser Printing House, 1872. Library of Congress, portfolio 134, folder 13, https://www.loc.gov/item/rbpe.13401300/.

9. A pile of American bison skulls waiting to be ground for fertilizer, mid-1870s. Wikimedia Commons, Burton Historical Collection, Detroit Public Library.

10. Buried machinery in barn lot in Dallas, South Dakota, May 1936. Wikimedia Commons, U.S. Department of Agriculture, oodio971.

11. John Jacob Astor, full-length portrait, New York, ca. 1864. Library of Congress, Prints and Photographs Division, LC-USZ62–8247.

12. Theodore Roosevelt, 1885. Photograph by George Grantham Bain. Library of Congress, Prints and Photographs Division, LC-USZ 62–23232.

13. William T. Hornaday, director of the Zoological Park of the New York Zoological Society, who inaugurated the movements for the protection of the Wichita and Montana national bison herds. Wikimedia Commons, *American Museum Journal*, American Museum of Natural History, New York, 1825.

14. William F. "Buffalo Bill" Cody, ca. 1911. Library of Congress, Prints and Photographs Division, LC-USZ62–2050.

15. Young bull with older cow. Notice the thick, strong base of the bull's horns compared to the graceful curves of the cow's horns. The bull's horns evolved to fight other bulls, the cow's evolved to defend her calves. Photograph by Jill O'Brien.

16. Old herd bull with mature horns. Photograph by Jill O'Brien.

17. Cow with "golden" calf. The calf's coat will turn dark brown like its mother's at about four months of age. Photograph by Jill O'Brien.

18. Yearling mingling with herd. Photograph by Jill O'Brien.

19. Winter herd watering at the Cheyenne River in the shadow of Stronghold Table. Photograph by Jill O'Brien.

20. Ninety percent of all buffalo produced for meat spend the last few months of their lives in desolate feedlots that force buffalo to contribute to the destruction of their own habitat. Courtesy of Energy & Environmental Research Center.

CHAPTER FIVE

The Old Switcheroo

The Second Wave

After the last ghost dance there was a period of years when the domain of the buffalo fell silent. There was no pounding of buffalo herds moving from one river drainage to the next. No roaring during mating season. No clouds of dust from buffalo wallowing in the heat of summer. Of course the westward wave of Euro-Americans continued, gaining speed—washing over the plains. In a matter of a few decades, much of the life within the ecosystem of the Great Plains had begun to disappear.

The last years of the free-ranging buffalo was a time of intense change in America. Bracketed between the rebellion of the slaveholding states and World War I, America was ebullient as a precocious teenager. Progress was the word of the day, and a belief in a God-given right to expand the boundaries of the United States from the Atlantic to the Pacific Oceans drove development of the Great Plains at a fever pitch. The few buffalo that remained—hiding in high mountains where they would never have chosen to live or desperately on the run across their disappearing prairies—were mostly invisible. When Americans looked at the Great Plains all they saw was potential for mindless, gung-ho agriculture—an immense opportunity to turn a profit.

The buffalo and many of the furbearers would soon be gone,

and because the other hundreds of species that depended on those keystone species had no obvious monetary value, no one bothered to learn much about them. No one cared about prairie dogs, butterflies, ground-nesting birds, rodents, or mustelids. They learned just enough about the big predators to kill them outright—as a precaution against the damage they might do when settlers finally filled the land. The United States was laying its claim to being the most innovative, productive nation on Earth. In fact, the "progress" that was making the United States the envy of the world was greatly dependent on the exploitation of virgin landscapes. Americans proudly pointed to high revenues while ignoring much of the true cost.

By 1900 almost fifteen million immigrants had already come to the United States. A substantial percentage of them passed through or took up residence on the Great Plains. Many more would come to the Great Plains in the first few decades of the twentieth century. Most were escaping wars and famines in Europe, and it is easy to understand why the promise of landownership and a fresh start attracted them. But some left fairly stable livelihoods in Europe or the eastern part of the United States to roll the dice on a windy farm in Kansas or on the frozen rangeland of North Dakota. Many homesteaders on the Great Plains tired quickly of poor harvests, freezing winters, and incessant wind. They moved on to less hostile places like Oregon, Washington, and California or back to where they came from.

Because, in the days before Columbus, America was spared the social rigidity and economic appetites of Europe, it had, to a large extent, been able to keep human dominance to manageable ecological levels. It looked like a backward country to the Europeans who "discovered" it. But in reality, it was a much more ecologically balanced country than Europe had been for many centuries. When the European mind beheld this continent it was capable of appreciating America only as a huge, untapped resource. The great powers of Europe took their turns at controlling and exploiting those resources, and as they did, they took their turns at world dominance. When the United States was founded, at the end of the eighteenth century, the new nation claimed those resources and, in the fashion of Europeans, converted them into an ascendency to world power. The power of present-day America was spawned from the modus operandi of a tired Europe whose rich-and-powerful class had exhausted its vitality and resources. When Europe's impoverished overflow of people came to the buffalo kingdom, they figured it was finally their turn to make their own claims to wealth and power.

Among the thousands of U.S. patents filed in the nineteenth century, a surprising number have a direct relationship to changing the face of the Great Plains—the self-polishing plow, the repeating rifle, the jackhammer, the grain elevator, Morse code, the steam shovel, the pipe wrench, the combine harvester, the cowboy hat, the machine gun, the ratchet wrench, the silo, the oil burner, the metal detector, blue jeans, the corn sheller, the cash register. There were also a myriad of railroad-connected inventions, bridge truss designs, mining techniques, and hay processing equipment, as well as barbed wire.

With few large, wild grazing animals left, Mexican and American ranchers, backed by foreign bankers, began to gather huge herds of escaped Spanish longhorn cattle and move them onto the ranges that had once belonged to the now-extirpated buffalo. As the railroads crept westward, shipping points on the Great Plains began to appear on the open prairie that were accessible to the herds coming up from the south. Links were completed between the Mexican cattle on the plains and slaughter plants in eastern cities—particularly Chicago. Herds numbering in the thousands moved north on the same trails that buffalo had used only a few years before. But the cattle-men were not simply driving their stock to market. They had discovered that the grass of the northern ranges was tremen-dously nutritious and their cattle could benefit greatly in terms of total salable pounds if they could spend time fattening on those plains. Getting them there was not easy, and there were still some areas that were being disputed by Indians, but the potential profits were worth the risks.

Following the European model, the grasslands of the Great Plains were seen by Americans as an enormous commons—an open area associated with a population center, where all citizens had the right to graze their cattle. Unlike the European ver-sion, this commons was bigger than many European countries. The buffalo kingdom was considered the property of the U.S. government; until it was portioned out, it could theoretically be used by any American citizen. Very quickly, though, the ownership of resources such as timber, minerals, and water found its way back into control by government officials or into the exclusive hands of privileged individuals. The grass that sustained the huge buffalo herds was finally considered a resource after the Indians were decimated and it became safe for stockmen to move in their herds of sheep and cattle.

Because of the size of this "commons," only men with enough wealth to mobilize huge herds and crews of men could play in this new, very American, game. At first the money came from Europe: England, Scotland, Germany, France. Often it was a syndicate of wealthy men who got together to bankroll an enormous operation of many thousand head of livestock and scores of poor herders in a land that many of the princi-pals had never seen. The money was used to buy cattle, make payroll for the cowboys, and pay for a little development of infrastructure—but the land was free. Now that the buffalo were gone, hundreds of thousands of square miles of land was available to men who could afford to stock it. Moving a few thousand head of cattle onto a range that had been recently cleared of buffalo must have been an amazing undertaking. To drive cattle from south Texas to Montana was to tour the buffalo kingdom from south to north—viewing it through the ears of a saddle horse. The first to make the trip talked of the eerie sensation of moving across mile after mile of empty land. It was a kind of graveyard, with the bones of buffalo lying in every direction.

No one imagined that the lack of buffalo could eventually create a trophic cascade of extinction that would negatively affect almost every species on the Great Plains. The cattlemen saw only an opportunity to make money, and for a few years, they did.

The northern Great Plains proved to be capable of fattening hundreds of thousands of cattle, readying them for shipment to eastern markets. The cattle were simply let loose to move like pitiful buffalo substitutes. They would mix with the cattle of other cattlemen, whose cowboys would keep a casual eye on them—most ranges consisting of hundreds of square miles of unpeopled land. In the fall as many cattle as possible were rounded up, and each cattleman would cut off the ones with his brand that were large enough to ship and sell. The profits were enormous, and the cattle business boomed. First it was a live cattle market with railroads stretching out to points across Nebraska, the Dakotas, and Montana. Some of the same trains that had hauled buffalo hides to the east now hauled live cattle. The steers that had fattened for a year or two on the hardy perennial grasses moved to slaughter plants in Chicago, Kansas City, Omaha, Toronto, and other eastern cities until Gustavus Swift invented the refrigerated railcar in 1878.

For wealthy men in the nineteenth century, and perhaps for all men at all times, there was something alluring about shooting a buffalo. In the case of Theodore Roosevelt the allure was irresistible. There is no question that Roosevelt was one of America's greatest conservationists, but like many conservationists, he was also a great hunter. These are the people who actually get out into the wilds and give that experience the benefit of their energy and intellect. These are the people who realize that conservation in the largest sense is concerned with species and the habitat where they live. The individual within the species, though important for other reasons, seldom has much to do with conservation. In the case of Teddy Roosevelt and his 1883 buffalo hunt, the species and the individual were dangerously close to being the same thing. During the hunt, Roosevelt managed to kill the buffalo that he coveted. He was a nearly fanatical proponent of ethics in hunting and all relationships toward animals, but his poor shooting makes one wonder if he was capable of suspending his ethics in the middle of the chase—he fired repeatedly from the ground and from horseback, crippling and finally bringing down his prey.

Roosevelt, who to that point in life had been only a wealthy Harvard boy who had risen to the position of representative in the New York State Assembly, seems to have found his life's direction on the plains of western Dakota Territory. When he returned to New York it was to arrange for the purchase of the Maltese Cross Ranch in what is now southwestern North Dakota. He would soon buy another ranch in that area, which he named the Elkhorn Ranch. Though for the next few years he spent every spare moment on those properties, his life changed course with his connection to the northern Plains and pointed him in the direction of the presidency of the United States. Among many other accomplishments—he would become a war hero, build the Panama Canal, and win a Noble Prize for negotiating a peace between China and Russia—he was also central in the effort to save the buffalo from extinction and became known as the "conservation president," directly responsible for affording federal protection to more land than any other president. It is probable that Roosevelt's experience hunting some of the last free-roaming buffalo led him to understand that, even considering all his achievements and accolades in the larger world, his work in conservation was his most enduring legacy.

Part of that legacy might well have been driven by his understanding of the limitations of the Great Plains. He learned firsthand that the climate of the Great Plains is capable of immense temperature swings—he watched the annual rainfall on his ranches vary from a throat-choking fraction of an inch to floods that pushed water for miles on either side of the once tranquil rivers. He was no armchair conservationist. He sweltered in the heat as he worked cattle on hundred-degree days. He shivered and fought frostbite. In the winter of 1888–89 a series of blizzards killed tens of thousands of cattle on the northern plains—including many of Roosevelt's—enough to end the era of open-range cattle ranching.

After realizing that free-range cattle were not like buffalo and would not work on the northern plains, many cattle ranchers simply pulled out. They were not leaving much. Few had built much in the way of infrastructure, and they had almost no investment in land; they had spent their money on cattle, and after that fateful winter, most of them were dead. But a few ranchers altered their approach to raising cattle and held on. They gathered up what cattle they could find, built buildings and corrals, invested in hay-mowing machines and hay-stacking equipment. They traded off a few of their cow ponies for workhorses and began turning the wild grass to hay to feed their cattle in the wintertime.

In 1867 the first patent was granted for an invention that would do more to change the function of the buffalo kingdom than anything since the destruction of the buffalo themselves.

When the experiment of open-range cattle failed, the ranches of the Great Plains began to be circled with barbed wire. From that day forward almost nothing on the Great Plains was truly wild. The large grazing animals were not allowed to move, and that changed everything. Now the grazers were confined to relatively small areas. Cattle were "turned out" into larger, fenced, upland pastures in the summertime. If the weather on a given ranch was good and the grass grew well, the cattle got fat and the rancher put up tons of hay. The calves were sold in the fall and the rancher made money. Once the calves were gone the cows would be moved into smaller pastures near the permanent buildings that the rancher had been forced to construct, so they could be fed over the winter. If the summer had been dry and the grass didn't grow there was no chance for the cattle to move to better pasture, as the buffalo had done. Barbed wire blocked their escape.

And then there was the problem of what to do with all the calves. Suddenly hundreds of thousands of young cattle were available to be raised and fattened for slaughter. A secondary business developed. The yearling operation took the calves and moved them to different barbed wire–fenced pastures with drovers or by railroads. Separating the cows from the calves was a new concept. In the open-range days cattle survived more like buffalo. The calves were allowed to stay with their mothers and herds until they were at least two years old before they were cut off and sold for slaughter. When the open-range days ended the need to take special care of the weaned calves began. This meant that more feed had to be produced in the form of grain. The topsoil had to be turned root-side-up, and the native perennial plants began to die out as annual grains were planted in their place. In those days no one thought much about the hundreds of species of plants and animals that needed those unplowed prairies for survival. It would be another fifty years before mankind would realize that the dense underground root masses of those perennial grasses were holding billions of tons of carbon in the soil and that plowing released that carbon into the atmosphere and created a problem that dwarfed any human problem ever imagined.

While the Great Plains were being fenced with barbed wire and the perennial grasses were being destroyed with steel plows, the few remaining buffalo were still being harassed by wealthy adventurers, hungry Indians, and market hunters. From early on, conservationists had been decrying the slaughter of buffalo, but their voices had been ignored or shouted down by those with a vested interest in the hide trade and the destruction of Indians that would lead to gaining control of natural resources in the West. Even as the main slaughter was still taking place on the southern plains, states and territories were beginning to pass legislation to protect buffalo. Those laws were mostly lip service to appease the conservationists, because most of the legislation applied to areas where there never were many buffalo or where nonviable numbers were left. More importantly, none of the laws had provisions for effective enforcement, so the slaughter continued unimpeded.

An 1889 census conducted by the Smithsonian Institution's William Hornaday estimated that only about 1,091 buffalo remained. One of the refuges that the buffalo retreated to was the high country that, in 1872, had become Yellowstone National Park. It never was ideal buffalo country, but in the last decade of the nineteenth century its remoteness discouraged poachers. Administration of the park bounced between territorial, state, and federal control, and finally policing fell to the U.S. Cavalry. Still, there was no regulation concerning the few besieged buffalo, and market hunters continued to prey on them. In the winter of 1893–94 a poacher named Howell was detained inside Yellowstone National Park after troopers caught him in the act of killing Yellowstone buffalo. On the way back to the park guardhouse at Mammoth Hot Springs, the troopers with their detainee came across a group of conservationists touring the park. One of the conservationists was a correspondent for *Forest and Stream* magazine and another was a photographer. They got the story and some pictures of the poacher and the remains of the buffalo he had killed. There was no law or regulation against the killing of buffalo on federal land, and so the troopers took Howell to civil authorities in nearby Wyoming, where a toothless law had recently been enacted.

It turned out that there was no provision for a poacher caught on federal land to be transported to a state for punishment, so Howell had to be released. *Forest and Stream* published an article about the incident, along with graphic pictures, and the East Coast erupted in indignation. Within the year Representative John F. Lacey of Iowa (where buffalo had been exterminated only fifty years before) introduced a bill providing for jail time and heavy fines for killing buffalo in Yellowstone National Park. The bill was passed and signed into law on May 7, 1894. It was the first federal legislation of its kind and came a half century too late for millions of buffalo.

CHAPTER SIX

Penning the Prairie

The Third Wave

There are no reports of any buffalo dying during the winter of 1888, but by then there were barely enough left to notice. The tough old stragglers could dig down through the ice and snow to find enough forage to survive. If not, they likely moved away from the terrible winter. They might have moved hundreds of miles before they found a place to winter safely. They were a super race of buffalo who had been honed by seventy years of intense selection for wildness and fear of humans. The docile beasts that the Indians remembered and early Europeans found when they first came to the prairies were gone. What remained were traumatized veterans who would run crazily at the first sight of man. They became phantom animals that would seek out remote valleys where they could hide all day and graze at night. In another sense, the true buffalo, since about 1860, had been hiding in the genes of those disparate refugees. Inside each of those turn-of-the-century buffalo, and indeed all buffalo that exist today, was the will and the ability to move to where survival is easiest. The closing of the land by settlement and particularly by the construction of flimsy cattle fences changed neither their desire nor their ability to move as they had always moved. Two- or three-strand barbed wire fences were not an adequate barrier—the lead buffalo jumped over them and the ones behind went through them.

The last decades of the nineteenth and first half of the twentieth centuries saw an explosion of immigrant settlement as the open-range cattle culture folded and homesteaders moved onto the fertile but dry plains. The railroad industry pushed ahead with its scheme of promising services to would-be communities across the prairie. It stretched rail service to all parts of America, including remote regions of the Great Plains. The plan was actually a swindle because very few of those planned communities actually amounted to anything more than a place for the steam trains to fill their water tanks and load up with coal. Shameful speculation in waterless land was rampant as the immigrants tackled the sometimes impossible task of building homes in the old buffalo kingdom.

Settlers in that early wave were too ineffectual to raise decent crops in the droughts that were inevitable, but as they dried out and moved on, more entrepreneurial farmers bought their farms, applied the power of the Industrial Revolution to destroying the grasses of the plains, and began to successfully raise grain from the virgin ground. They also set about demarcating their land in earnest.

The surveying of land in the New World had started with the first Europeans who stepped onto the North American continent. Those early Americans chose a system of landownership that they understood from the common laws of Europe—especially England—called fee simple ownership. I first learned of this way of looking at land from my father. We had a little farm that was my own, private ecological playground into which I disappeared every chance I got. It was only two hundred acres, and when I grew to my teenage years I began to range out farther and farther—until I reached the boundary of the farm. My father sat me down at our kitchen table and told me that I was not allowed to go onto the neighbor's land.

"You don't have that right," he said. Then he explained about the sections, townships, and counties that the entire nation is divided into. He drew a little map of our farm and showed me the land that the neighbors owned.

"Where is the land that belongs to nobody?" I asked.

He looked at me curiously. "There is no land like that," he said.

That was the day I learned that our system dictates that every square inch of land must belong to, and be controlled by, some human being or group of human beings. The rights to dwell upon, protect, and profit from all land are inherent in fee simple ownership, and so before any commerce could take place in America, the land had to be measured and noted in the public record. Now, I am embarrassed that I was a teenager before I understood that. For contemporary Americans it is difficult to fathom that there is any other system of landownership, but in fact there are several other ways to look at land—from total ownership by a monarch to the loose common ownership that Indians and buffalo practiced. The adoption and wide use of barbed wire was, in part, an attempt to finally establish and enshrine fee simple landownership on the Great Plains. The unintended (or perhaps it was intended) consequence was to end the freedom of movement that had always been the hallmark of the Great Plains.

Barbed wire was a Great Plains invention born from the nascent need to enclose land without the typical fencing materials of wood and stones, which were lacking beyond the hundredth meridian. With barbed wire, large areas could be fenced in a short period of time at a reasonable cost. In 1901 a single company sold 248,669 tons of the stuff at prices that were affordable to almost everyone. The result was that by midcentury perhaps a billion miles of barbed wire stretched across the Great Plains. The entire buffalo kingdom was fenced and cross fenced. Not only did all that fencing bring the era of free-range cattle ranching to an end, it also put the last nail in the coffin of the wild buffalo. Regular cattle fence could not contain the few survivors of the great buffalo pogrom. But even if the buffalo jumped over or tore down the fences, they were still contained—guilty of trespassing on private, fee simple land. The new human society on the Great Plains could not abide the destruction of private property. Damage done to the fences and the grass that was "stolen" by the buffalo's grazing were offenses that could not be tolerated. After barbed wire came to the Great Plans all the buffalo that were left were effectively, and for the reasonably foreseeable future, constrained inside a fence and a foreign system of landownership. They were, nearly by definition, felons for being buffalo.

No one had experience growing crops in this dry land, but often for the first year or so after the ancient perennial grasses were plowed under and small grain was planted, the harvests were good. The main reason for the initially good crop years was that the soil beneath the protecting grass that was plowed under had been storing nutrients and conserving water for eons. When the homesteaders planted their seed, they were benefiting from the very process that they were destroying. Such experiences encouraged the novice farmers to plow more. But after the fertility and moisture of newly plowed land was used up, crop yields began to fall off drastically. At the turn of the twentieth century Great Plains farmers would farm fields until they played out. Because they were destroying the perennial grasses that had evolved to hold moisture in the soil through dry periods, the land was depleted even faster. But they had mortgaged their farms to pay for equipment and supplies. They couldn't stop, the bank wouldn't let them, and so they simply plowed up another patch of native grass. Soon they had plowed all the land they owned, destroying all of the stored nutrients. The Great Plains, now nearly devoid of buffalo and crawling with poor farmers, went through several cycles of boom and bust before the mother of all busts hit in the 1930s.

By then the homestead farmer had nearly disappeared like the buffalo. The land had been gobbled up by more serious farmers, early corporations, and absentee investors with access to capital and friends in Washington DC. Grand new inventions promised more efficiency and more profit. New wonder-machines were coming off the assembly lines in the East and they promised more profit. Tractors that could pull with the power of many horses. The old walk-behind plows were replaced with gang plows with multiple blades, then plows with wheels and seats for the operator, massive plows pulled by the ever more powerful tractors, and finally battalions of tractor-powered steel plows designed specifically for rolling over the prairie sod that was the bedrock of Great Plains life. To complement these enormous grass destroyers came the first large-scale reaping and thrashing machines, and then, in 1910, horse-drawn combine harvesters came onto the scene and the two basic harvesting functions were joined into one process. Soon steam or gas power was adapted for the combines and the tilling equipment. While these machines might have made sense for some areas of America, where water was plentiful and winter was short, they were abusive to the ocean of grass that was the old buffalo kingdom. As if flaying a human body, they stripped the land of its protective cover and destroyed its fertility. The results were inevitable.

Dryland farming amounted to a full-scale assault on the soul of the Great Plains. The only missing element was a decent price for the wheat that could be produced. The turmoil and war that erupted in Europe in the 1910s supplied that element, and the rush to capitalize on the obliteration of the Great Plains was on.

In 1914, when World War I began, wheat was selling in North Dakota for 64 cents a bushel. By the war's end in 1920, with France, England, and Belgium crying for bread, the price of wheat had jumped to $2.45 per bushel. This price increase of over 380 percent was enough to stimulate an assault on the buffalo kingdom equivalent to but even more permanent than the slaughter of the buffalo themselves. Millions of additional acres were plowed and laid naked to the persistent dry winds that descended on the Great Plains in the 1930s. By 1932 the price of wheat had fallen to 49 cents and people were suffering economic collapse, starvation, and displacement not seen since the buffalo had disappeared sixty years before.

The few hundred buffalo that were left from the herds of many millions were hiding in the mountains or under the protection of a few progressive ranchers or government agencies. From behind high, strong, barbed, electrified, or woven wire fences, from inaccessible mountains, or from country too rough for humans to follow them, the buffalo helplessly watched what was happening to their land. They had seen many droughts during their dominance of the Great Plains. Such dryness had been a standard feature of the land since the Rocky Mountains rose up and the oceans receded to approximately their present locations. These droughts were a major factor in the evolution of the plants that dominated the land and that the buffalo thrived on, but those specially evolved plants were diminished from the abuse of plows and overgrazing of domestic animals.

As twentieth-century industrial farmers got serious about making huge war profits they were also setting the Great Plains up for a catastrophe that periodic normal droughts had never before visited upon the Great Plains. Once the grassy, protective covering of the fragile soil was stripped away and the inevitable dry winds began to blow, the land began to move. In *The Dust Bowl: An Agricultural and Social History*, R. Douglas Hurt pins down the time and immediate reason for the Dust Bowl: "It was the rapid expansion of wheat production following World War I that destroyed the soil-holding native grasses and created the Dust Bowl. After drought ruined the wheat crop during the autumn of 1931, the prevailing winds began to lift the soil and plague the region with dust storms by late January of 1932."

It may be more than coincidental that a map of the Dust Bowl's heart almost exactly outlines the area inhabited by the great southern buffalo herd of the 1860s—southeastern Colorado, western Oklahoma and Kansas, the panhandle of Texas, parts of Nebraska, and the far northeastern portion of New Mexico. When the buffalo were extinguished from that land, devastation and gross loss of fertility followed close behind. Dust Bowl conditions spread into the land of the northern herd, too, but because of ongoing Indian wars and the resulting huge Indian reservations, farming was restricted and buffalo remained on the land for a couple more decades. Though drought was serious in the northern buffalo range, conditions never reached the apocalyptic levels experienced in the south.

The Dust Bowl was the beginning of a final insult to the buffalo's landscape. Like an invading nation burning the crops and poisoning the wells of a conquered nation, America rendered a large portion of the buffalo kingdom nearly unusable for many years to come. Many of the last settlers had to move away from the hardest-hit areas of the Dust Bowl. By the beginning of the 1940s only a few small-scale farmers remained active.

The people who made it through the Dust Bowl—from the day-labor farmers to eastern industrialist investors—were many things, but they were not quitters. Once the world had settled down from the 1930s, World War II quickly followed. The exploiters of the Great Plains used that second twentieth-century war as justification for the renewed conquest of the buffalo kingdom.

CHAPTER SEVEN

The Unintended Consequences of Technology

The Fourth Wave

Even before World War I, buffalo were effectively out of the picture in America. That war, and the one that followed twenty years later, intensified the pressure to create on the Great Plains a future that was radically different from the past that had served humans for tens of thousands of years. This new vision did not include buffalo. The difference between the past and the future visions of the Great Plains was wrapped up in the differences between hunting and farming, nomadic and sedentary culture, living with and fighting against nature. At its core, the new thrust of humans on the Great Plains would be to achieve a kind of pastoral paradise through the use of technology. The first step had been to clear the stage, and that meant getting rid of the buffalo and their Indian cousins. That task was mostly finished by 1900, but to completely change the nature of the Great Plains was a job even more massive than the near extermination of a couple of species. A string of perceived problems would have to be overcome: lack of people, lack of soil fertility, lack of water, lack of suitable crops, and a plethora of pests that preyed upon and competed with the crops that were intended to cover the land.

To the European mind, the Great Plains always seemed empty. Of course, this was a misconception, the Great Plains were always full of life, but it was the kind of life that was not centered on human beings, and that troubled the early pioneers, religious people, industrialists, and developers. The drive to expand the numbers of humans and their store of material goods was in full swing by the first decades of the twentieth century. If America, and indeed the entire world, was to double, triple, quadruple its human population it would need more human food. A good way to do that would be to increase the fertility of land that was flat enough to farm, and that included the Great Plains of North America.

Nitrogen makes things grow; the atmosphere is 80 percent nitrogen, but nitrogen in the air is not directly accessible to plants. There are some plants that suck it out of the air and deposit it in the ground, where other plants can use it to grow verdant and tall. Unfortunately, during the settlement of the Great Plains, most native nitrogen-fixing plants were not deemed particularly useful for humans and, if they were considered at all, they were usually considered weeds and destroyed where possible. Besides, they could never produce the volume of nitrogen fertilizer that would be needed to convert the prairies to farm fields.

The solution to the Great Plains' fertility problem came from experiments with military munitions during the twentieth-century wars. A nearly endless supply of nitrogen fertilizer was found by two German scientists—Fritz Haber and Carl Bosch—in their quest to supply their country with enough explosives to wage worldwide war. The chemical difference between nitrogen for fertilizer and nitrite for TNT is small, and once Haber figured out a way to extract nitrogen from the air Bosch went to work industrializing the procedure. The Haber-Bosch process was demonstrated in the lab in 1909, and by the beginning of World War II the combatants were producing millions of pounds of TNT annually—enough to destroy many of Europe's cities and kill millions of people. A great irony was that both Haber and Bosch won a Nobel Prize in Chemistry in the years leading up to World War II.

But, in an even greater irony, we now produce about five hundred million tons of nitrogen fertilizer per year, and though much of it is intended to increase land fertility, it is dramatically decreasing the biodiversity of the old buffalo kingdom by spreading industrial monoculture farming across the Great Plains and poisoning most of the waterways on the continent. When Europeans first set foot in the New World they found a phenomenally diverse ecosystem where a human could drink freely from almost any stream. The nitrogen fertilizer that was a byproduct from the Haber-Bosch process was more lastingly devastating to the Great Plains than the nitrite bombs were to European cities.

Through a system of state, federal, and territorial water laws every creek, stream, lake, river, and underground aquifer in the Great Plains was assigned to owners—sometimes local men and women trying to improve their little farms, but more often to wealthy absentee developers. Every water source that the buffalo had freely drunk from now belonged to some human being or group of human beings and was undrinkable for humans without expensive treatment. Beginning with rivers and the water from snow runoff, America went about the job of cataloging, containing, and developing the water of the Great Plains. Most of it was allocated for agricultural use, but some went for flood control, recreation, and power generation.

The Ogallala Aquifer is an ocean of water that underlies 174,000 square miles of the Great Plains. The amount of water in the aquifer is estimated by the U.S. Geological Survey to be about three billion acre-feet. (An acre-foot is the amount of water needed to cover one acre of land to a depth of one foot.) It is one of the world's largest reservoirs of fresh water, with a storage capacity so large that rainfall could not have filled it.

Instead, the water in the Ogallala Aquifer is ancient—mostly ice melt from the last ice age. It is part of a system of aquifers that are interconnected to rivers and streams from South Dakota to the panhandle of Texas—tracing the bulk of the area that once supported all of the southern buffalo herd and part of the northern herd.

Beginning in the 1940s farmers began to tap the Ogallala Aquifer to supply irrigation water for their newly created fields of corn, beans, and wheat where perennial grasses had grown successfully, without irrigation, for many thousands of years. At first things worked well, but after World War II, when farming began to become an industry, the water levels in the Ogallala began to fall. The first water sources to go were at the top of the aquifer, where the rivers touch the surface. At first farmers believed it was just the normal cycle of Great Plains drought that was making the rivers go dry but soon it became apparent that irrigation was lowering the water level in the aquifer.

According to a *New York Times* article from 2013, Kansas alone has over three million acres of irrigated corn watered from probably fifteen thousand circle irrigators pumping hundreds and sometimes thousands of gallons of water per minute. The result of this level of irrigation throughout the Great Plains has been a decline of at least 10 percent of the total storage volume of the Ogallala Aquifer since the 1950s, and the depletion is accelerating at an increasing rate. Many of the rivers where the buffalo once watered are now dry. The playa lakes that also represented the top of the aquifer are now plowed over to plant more corn. Perhaps the most outrageous water boondoggle of all time is the planned theft of water from beneath those playa lakes by the oil tycoon T. Boone Pickens. He has finagled the rights to the Ogallala Aquifer and plans to pump water from under the southern Great Plains to Dallas, Fort Worth, Houston, and cities beyond.

Many water projects have been too large even for individuals like T. Boone Pickens to finance. In such cases, federal or state governments collaborated in the dream of turning arid lands into gardens. These schemes were often political boondoggles plagued with corruption, poor engineering, and incredible lack of foresight. Massive irrigation projects were often little more than government-subsidized favors for wealthy friends or vote-getting strategies aimed at the farmers or the promoters who would profit when cheap, dry land could be sold as irrigated farms. Many of these projects failed, and alteration of the natural flow of rivers and other watercourses damaged the land through erosion or the introduction of invasive plants that, when the grand projects finally went bankrupt, made repopulation by native plants and animals nearly impossible.

Even with the failures, these projects increased the annual harvests from America's agricultural sector. While a few developers and speculators were made rich, these projects never had the potential of making farmers rich. In fact, already-subsidized irrigated farms were soon doubly subsidized with similar government programs available to dryland famers. In a perversion of the economic system that spawned them, the upshot of these government programs was to take the risk out of farming. Capitalism cannot function without risk, and the farmers were on their way to becoming wards of the state. This system of government support was intended to keep people on the land, and to a large extent, it did. But among the unintended consequences was that the farmers were tied hard and fast to the land by bank payments and poverty and were supported by nonfarm taxpayers.

As the Great Plains was converted from a polyculture of many hundreds of plants that thrived in arid and semiarid grasslands to a few monocultures that needed continuous applications of human technology, the insects that had been held in check by the biodiversity of the plains moved into the void. No longer did the natural mosaic of different plants limit the effect of pests by dispersing their favorite plants and making serious infestation nearly impossible.

Since the beginning of time humans have been locked in combat with insects. Bugs have bitten them, bothered them, infected them with diseases, and eaten their crops. And humans, for their part, have fought them with slaps, smoke, dislocation, skin ointments, and grumbled oaths. The wide use of atomizer sprayers in the early years of the twentieth century made the use of lead- and arsenic-based sprays for killing insects feasible for small areas such as homes and livestock facilities, but when insects began to invade the immense new grain fields of the Great Plains in the middle decades of the twentieth century the battle escalated. DDT is a synthetic insecticide that was developed by a Swiss scientist named Paul Müller in 1944 and aimed mostly toward the eradication of mosquitoes. When it was discovered that DDT would kill an array of insect pests that plagued monoculture crops like those recently introduced to the Great Plains, the chemical was sprayed wholesale.

Why we thought that a synthetic compound that replaced lead- and arsenic-based sprays was harmless is hard to understand. Certainly we wanted a product that would kill only targeted insects, and the corporations that produced DDT encouraged that hope. But of course there is no Santa Claus, and there is no way to kill a single species without affecting all the other species. The unintended consequence of spraying insecticides was to kill insects indiscriminately. The insect world is a major pillar of almost every ecosystem and is of paramount importance on the Great Plains. The destruction of insects and insect diversity delivered a serious blow to all the flowering plants that the buffalo kingdom had once been famous for. The pollinators of these plants were attacked, and great monoculture fields that had once been rich with diversity became biodeserts. The devastation created by the use of D D T and similar pesticides also reached into the avian world and the world of mammals. Rachel Carson blew the whistle on pesticides in her book *Silent Spring*. The result of the outcry would eventually lead to a nearly worldwide ban on D D T and its ilk. But in the meantime (and for decades after the ban) the birds that ate infected insects—and the birds that ate those birds—laid eggs with shells too thin to hatch, causing bird populations to plummet. D D T is still detected in our food and in our bodies, and still we have little understanding of its ongoing damage.

Insects were not the only opportunistic life-form to capitalize on changes that humans brought to the Great Plains. Like insects and rust, weeds never sleep. They are programmed to fill any opening where other plants are absent. Anyone who has ever tried to garden knows the determination of bindweed, wild lettuce, and burdock. Most invasive species were brought to North America in bags of seed and, purposefully or incidentally, planted in the New World where they had no natural enemies and lots of room to grow.

During World War II, in both the United States and the United Kingdom, programs to develop chemical weapons also produced aerosols that could kill plants. Those compounds were quickly adopted by the budding agriculture industry. This new technology was turned against what humans considered weeds and, in the case of the buffalo kingdom, any plant that competed with farmed crops. The idea was to tweak the humans' killing compounds in such a way as to make them more selective killers—capable of killing unwanted plants while not harming the desirable plants. This idea was embraced by agriculturalists around the world but particularly on the Great Plains of America.

For those applications where the goal is to kill all plants except those being farmed, Monsanto invented a particularly potent compound called Roundup. (Its military brother is Agent Orange—developed to defoliate Vietnamese jungles.) The immense mixed-greens salad of the Great Plains that buffalo had evolved to eat was being destroyed and replaced with grain-producing plants that buffalo, even if they still existed in numbers and could fight through the barbed wire to get to them, were poorly equipped to digest. In addition, many of Roundup's targeted plants had once created habitat for ground-nesting birds and other indigenous creatures. With these plants gone, Great Plains species have suffered an enormous loss of habitat. Populations have crashed.

Through ignorance, greed, or a horrible cynicism, catastrophic destruction of insects and weeds and the closing of the land was heralded as progress. Another area of similar progress has been the improvement of crop seeds. For centuries mankind has been selectively breeding grains to reduce their height. In effect, the crops that migrated in burlap sacks to the Great Plains were dwarfs of once wild plants from other continents. The reason for the development of dwarfs was to direct the energy of the plant into the production of the seed head, and so increase the amount of grain produced per plant. By the time corn and wheat got to the Great Plains, from Mexico via Indian trade routes and importation from Europe and Asia via settlers, the seed heads were greatly developed and the heights of the plants were diminished, making the plants more productive and less vulnerable to the destructive prairie winds. But the reengineering of non–Great Plains grains was soon subjected to the steamroller of agricultural production, and companies like Pioneer and Prairie Valley began to cross individual plants to produce even more productive plants. The process is called hybridization, and the idea is to cross unrelated plants to create what is called hybrid vigor. It works great, except the offspring are often not fertile and so the time-honored practice of farmers saving some of their crop for seed to be planted the next year is rendered impossible. The farmer has to buy new seed every year—a disadvantage for the men and women on the land but a boon for the industry that produces the hybrid seed.

Very little of the grain that has replaced the native grass on the Great Plains goes to feed people. Most of it is used for ethanol and to fatten animals for slaughter—animals that contribute to our over-intake of fat and the maladies that accompany obesity. Contrary to popular belief, this system is only a few decades old. It arose from the need to get rid of excess grains grown with the help of government subsidies and now encompasses an industry that creates about thirty-three million "fat" cattle a year—a number roughly equivalent to the number of buffalo that roamed the same grasslands where the feedlots now stand. The feedlot industry is a massive factory system that is alien to historic husbandry. Still, there is huge money in an industry masquerading as a connector of humans to the land. Feedlots are not family farms.

My family and I are not crop farmers. We produce completely grass-fed buffalo, and so we are farmers of grass. We know that plowing up native grasses destroys an ancient ecosystem of plants and that the destruction cascades to the wild animals, birds, and insects. The plants of the healthy pastures pull CO_2 from the air and, with the help of some microbes in healthy soil, split the carbon (C) away from the oxygen (O_2) and deposit it in the ground, where it can't create havoc in the atmosphere and cause climate change. As a happy side effect, the native grasses expire those two severed atoms of oxygen and make them available for us to breathe. The reason that the native perennial grasses do such a good job of this nifty trick is that sometimes 90 percent of a perennial plant's mass is below the surface of the soil. It doesn't die in the winter. It keeps growing every year, and carbon—sucked from the air—builds with the root system. Of course, when someone plows up such a plant and root system and replaces it with an annual plant that lives for only part of one year and has no time to build an extensive root system, the ability to sequester carbon in the soil is reduced by a huge percentage. The fertility of the soil is hauled away in grain trucks each fall, and the carbon is released into the atmosphere.

Many people would disagree, but one of the lucky things about the American Great Plains is that, for the first hundred years of settlement, there was seldom enough rain to grow grain. The Great Plains was always considered one of the world's greatest grasslands but a poor place to farm. From the time of the buffalo right up through the era of the cowboy it has nourished countless herbivores. Cattle, sheep, elk, antelope, and particularly buffalo grazed on the renewable grass, and the fertility and the carbon stayed in the ground where they belong. But now, in the first quarter of the twenty-first century, all that is changing.

As I have already said, farming is about nurturing a single kind of plant and destroying all other plants that can compete with that chosen plant. In places like the Great Plains, where moisture is in short supply, a farmer's job is to make sure that the crop he chooses to grow gets as much of the rainfall as is possible. On most of the Great Plains, crops do not have enough water to grow unless all the competition is killed. Many twentieth-century agricultural maps have a precipitation line on about the one hundredth meridian that marks the frontier of profitable dryland farming. Until recently, respect for that line saved the middle and western Great Plains' grasses that harbored most of the living things, pumped oxygen into the air, and sequestered billions of tons of carbon each year.

The use of plant killers like Roundup moved the precipitation line a little bit to the west, where the climate was drier, but lack of rainfall still managed to keep farming from completely destroying huge portions of the old buffalo kingdom. Then came genetically modified organisms—GMOs.

In the late twentieth century, scientists found a way to change the genetic makeup of certain crops so that Roundup, and other chemicals normally poisonous to all plants, had no effect on these genetically modified crops but killed everything else. This process dramatically increased yields by destroying the "weeds," not only before the crops were planted but after they were growing too. As usual, the innovation was lauded as a miracle that would help the world produce much more food. GMOs, Roundup-resistant crops, not only increased yields of existing cropland but expanded farming into areas where it had never before been economically feasible to produce crops because there was never enough rainfall to grow crops *and* "weeds." All of a sudden the precipitation line that had protected the grass resources of our continent was pushed westward. In one generation it became profitable to grow farm crops by plowing up healthy grasslands, even in arid and semiarid landscapes.

GMO crops have been criticized for many reasons. Some call them Frankenstein plants, complete with the allusions of monster plants creeping out of laboratories to prey on unsuspecting life-forms. Others are concerned about GMOs' ability to cross-pollinate with "normal" plants. Certainly they destroy biodiversity by creating sterile monocultures where nothing grows but the chosen GMO plant. They have been called the harbinger of a new silent spring, and many worry about their effect on the animals and humans consuming the grain that they produce. There are also legal questions about the ownership of seeds produced by GMOs—do they belong to the farmer who bought them or to the chemical companies that created them?

It is hard to measure the validity of these concerns, but there is one concern that is undisputable—G M O farming threatens the biodiversity of our Great Plains by making possible the conversion of grasslands to croplands.

G M O technology makes profitable farming possible on the portion of our ranch called Phiney Flat and many other places on the Great Plains. It supplies an incentive for ranchers who still control healthy portions of the ancient buffalo kingdom to convert that grassland to cropland. Such conversion would render the return of meaningful numbers of buffalo impossible in the next many hundreds of years.

Though this will never happen to the portion of Phiney Flats that I control as long as I am alive, it is a temptation to which many will succumb. In addition to the windfall of government subsidies cash that one can claim for becoming a farmer, there is also a penalty for not making that deadly conversion. It is a little known fact that, in many Great Plains states, property taxes are calculated on the basis of a "best-use value," not an "actual-use value." What this means is that a ranch is taxed based on what the income could be if the land were plowed up and planted to G M O crops. Never mind the loss of biodiversity and fertility or the loss of carbon to the atmosphere. The tax differences are significant, and the margins in ranching are slim. There is no question that G M O agriculture is driving loss of grasslands, and those losses are not redeemable. This perfect storm of incentives and penalties is perhaps the greatest indictment against the use of genetically modified organisms. It could eventually be the final nail in the coffin of buffalo, and many other species, on the Great Plains. It is almost as if Big Agriculture and Big Government are working together, consciously or unconsciously, to ensure that buffalo, and the ecosystem that supported them, disappear from the face of Earth, forever.

It is certain that technology has and will continue to change the Great Plains. To paraphrase Richard Manning from his book *Against the Grain: How Agriculture Has Hijacked Civilization*, what was once one of the world's most productive grazing lands, meaning the production of a high-quality, low-cost source of protein, was sacrificed so that a low-quality, high-input, subsidized source of protein could blanket much of the old buffalo kingdom. It is as if we not only must kill the buffalo but must destroy all that might remind us of them. The thought of a stray buffalo bull looking down from a ridgetop at a construction site where hard-hatted engineers are directing the construction of giant steel grain bins is untenable. What if one wandered into the midst of a legion of bulldozers rechanneling a streambed? Best to destroy all trace.

But nature is a stubborn mother. Remnants of most Great Plains species persist. The Lakotas are still here, and they believe that the buffalo will someday return with dignity. They are not alone.

CHAPTER EIGHT

The Resistance

Creeping Back from the Shadows

Though there are some who question the story, the man who appears to have been the first to do something concrete about the looming loss of buffalo as a species was, perhaps predictably, an Indian. His name was Samuel Walking Coyote and he was from the Pend d'Oreille tribe of the Pacific Northwest. Apparently Walking Coyote, as his name suggests, was a traveling man. By 1872 he had migrated east to the land of the Flathead Indians and found a Flathead wife. The Jesuit fathers who were serving as missionaries with the Flatheads had blessed the union, though Walking Coyote had not bought fully into the idea of Christianity. He took off alone toward the northern Great Plains, where enough buffalo remained to hunt. He spent the winter of 1872–73 on the Blackfeet Reservation, where he must have become a little confused about the vows he took with the Flathead wife because he picked up a second wife, a lovely Blackfeet girl.

In the spring of 1873 he decided to head back to the Flathead Reservation, and he must have suspected that the Catholic fathers would not approve of the second wife because he brought a present for them. The fact that Walking Coyote thought the priests would accept his bribe of a little herd of orphaned buffalo calves is an insight into the high value he placed on buffalo.

He and his Blackfeet wife managed to get six of the eight calves over the Rocky Mountains and back to the Flathead Reservation, but the gift was scorned and the good fathers directed the reservation police to give both Walking Coyote and his second wife a sound beating. They limped away from the encounter with the six buffalo calves following behind. But Walking Coyote was nothing if not tenacious. He and the Blackfeet woman set up housekeeping at the most remote corner of the reservation and proceeded to create one of the very first buffalo ranches.

Ten years later Mr. and Mrs. Walking Coyote had a respectable little herd of thirteen buffalo with more being born every spring. Of course, Walking Coyote had no money for fences, and the buffalo began to roam onto the land of others. Finally, he was forced to sell his buffalo to a pair of successful local ranchers by the names of Charles Allard and Michel Pablo for $2,000 in gold. It was more money than Walking Coyote had ever seen, and he proceeded to burn through it. He died penniless under a bridge in Missoula, Montana. You could say he gave his life to keep the buffalo from vanishing.

With Allard and Pablo managing Walking Coyote's little herd, it grew by reproduction and acquisition of other buffalo. By 1895, when Allard died suddenly, the herd numbered about three hundred. At Allard's death the herd was split between Pablo's and Allard's relatives, who began to sell a few buffalo as seed stock for government and private herds across the Great Plains and beyond. Fifteen buffalo from Allard's share of the herd went to Yellowstone National Park to supplement the few survivors of the onslaught of poaching that had plagued the park in its early years.

Pablo's share of the herd continued to expand until 1906, when Pablo offered them for sale. He had built the herd back up to three hundred, and he wanted to sell the whole lot to the federal government. President Roosevelt agreed that the U.S. government would be the proper owner for this herd of buffalo and asked Congress for the money to buy them. But the Congress of the United States refused. Reluctantly, Pablo turned to the government of Canada, which bought them for $200 apiece, C O D at the railhead in Ravalli, Montana—about forty miles away. From there they would be shipped to Wainwright, Alberta, to form the seed stock for the Canadian prairies, which had lost nearly all of their native buffalo much as the American prairies had lost theirs. But to get paid Pablo had to get the buffalo to Ravalli, and they were scattered over many miles of poorly fenced rangeland. The cowboys he hired to round them up had no experience moving herds of buffalo. It took them six years to deliver the buffalo. By the time they were shipped to Canada there were seven hundred healthy American buffalo in the herd. They were finally shipped off to Canada, like so many refugees, where the Canadian government conducted experiments in an effort to turn them into draft animals and hybridize them with cattle. They never returned to their native country.

In the years when Allard and Pablo were building their herd, they bought a little band of buffalo from perhaps the most famous of the men who were dedicated to buffalo conservation in the nineteenth century. Charles Jessie "Buffalo" Jones was a Kansas jack-of-all-trades whose main trade was that of a hustler. Buffalo Jones was cut from the same stock as men like Buffalo Bill Cody and P. T. Barnum. These men realized that associating with charismatic animals would enhance their own, not insignificant, charismatic aura and would put dollars in their pockets. Jones was a sanctimonious showman, one of the West's first roadside hucksters, and one of the first to exploit buffalo for more than simply meat and hides.

By modern standards Buffalo Jones was an exploiter of

wildlife, but in the last half of the nineteenth century he was considered a conservationist. He was intelligent, energetic, gifted in handling animals, and an excellent cowboy. He was known for his skill as a roper, a craft that he parlayed into a career by first roping buffalo calves from the remnants of the southern herd and bringing them back to his ranch in northeastern Kansas, where he raised them with the help of milk cows. Later Jones developed land in Kansas and traveled the world collecting animals for zoos, but he is best known for his work with buffalo. He was one of the first to raise buffalo as semidomestic animals and made his first significant money by selling breeding stock to zoos and private ranchers.

Jones pioneered a technique that would be used by other buffalo calf capturers in the last decade of the truly wild herds. He took long horseback rides into country remote enough to hide remnants of the southern herd, and when he found buffalo with calves he rode down on a cow and her calf. From her experience, the cow would have learned that a rider coming hard meant death and she would take off at a full run. The calf would stick as close as it could but would soon tire. Jones stayed behind the mother until the calf was left a mile or so behind. Then Jones circled back and roped the calf, hiked it up on his saddle in front of him, and took it home to be grafted onto a gentle milk cow. Sometimes the baby calf was so confused that it would simply attach itself to the horse and follow it home. Jones gathered many calves this way, and almost all were adopted by the milk cows. Jones could move his newly acquired buffalo herd by simply moving the cows.

Other men up and down the Great Plains used variations of Jones's technique. Some did not bother to run the cow off and simply shot her before they roped the orphan. Men like the famous rancher Charles Goodnight of Texas and Pete Dupree, a mixed-blood rancher in the middle of South Dakota, began to build buffalo herds from remnant wild stock. Dupree was critical of the practice of men like Buffalo Jones and Charles Goodnight who mixed their buffalo with domestic cattle and tried to cross-breed them to create a super cow. Though the practice was never successful, it disgusted Dupree. He saw no reason to degrade buffalo by trying to make them more like cattle. Perhaps it was his Lakota heritage that enabled him to understand that it was an insult to the buffalo. But the craze of trying to create a breed of cattalo or beefalo, as they were called, took a brief hold on the men who controlled many of the privately owned buffalo in America and the buffalo managers of the Canadian government. These men were driven by a blend of arrogance, ignorance, and greed. They believed they could breed into cattle, in a few generations, the qualities of toughness, endurance, herd instinct, and intelligence that made buffalo the perfect grazer for the Great Plains. It had taken evolution tens of thousands of years to achieve this, so the attempt failed. The few hybrids that were produced were often infertile. The residue of that human fiddling with nature is still detectable in the buffalo gene pool, though it is being carefully winnowed out.

Buffalo Jones's association with buffalo brought him to national, and even international, fame, and he became acquainted with other notable conservationists of the time. Despite his flaws, he was responsible for supplying the seed stock for a weak but significant buffalo comeback. He was finally appointed by Theodore Roosevelt to be the first game warden of Yellowstone National Park and put in charge of building the park's buffalo herd.

About this time, the voices of reason that had been calling for the rescue and protection of a few buffalo were beginning to be heard by the public. These voices came from men and women of all segments of society but can better be categorized by geography. A small number were westerners who lived on the Great Plains and had actually seen free, wild buffalo—some in huge numbers—before the great killing hit its stride in the 1870s. Others were westerners who had made a little money from buffalo, some by exploiting them, but all felt a unique attraction toward and even a love for these deposed princes and princesses of a kingdom that was being destroyed. In several cases it was the wives and daughters of these men who were the arbitrators of their conscience. Walking Coyote's second wife showed her allegiance not only to Walking Coyote but also to the baby buffalo she had helped shepherd over the snow-covered Rocky Mountains. Charles Goodnight's wife appealed to Charlie's sense of decency and badgered him until he climbed back up on his Texas cow pony and rode out to bring in a batch of buffalo orphans. Pete Dupree and "Scotty" Philips lived with Indian women who, no doubt, encouraged them in attempting to make amends for what had happened to their people and, by extension, to the buffalo.

This small band of westerners was important, but most of the people who kept the buffalo species viable were not westerners. They were mainly wealthy, influential easterners whose connection to nature was academic or recreational—some had never even seen a live buffalo, let alone roped any buffalo calves from a horse or cared for a group of wild calves until they formed a small, semiwild herd. From the very beginning there were easterners who spoke out against the slaughter. Some clergymen and army officers bemoaned the waste and immorality of European and American behavior on the Great Plains. But the pressure to do something about the situation did not gain enough momentum to matter until it was almost too late.

By the last decade of the nineteenth century, those in the know were becoming panicked about the possibility of the entire species of American buffalo joining the ranks of dinosaurs and wooly mammoths. While man's hand in extinctions was not new, never before had a species' extinction been so obviously and completely the work of man. At the turn of the century scientists did not yet fully understand the connections between species within an ecosystem. They didn't know that the collapse of the buffalo would put the pressure of extinction on all the animals and plants in the ecosystem. It was not for scientific reasons that people began to speak out for saving the buffalo. It was a much more basic reason: There was something inspiring about buffalo that made people love them. People began speaking in defense of the buffalo as if they were a friend or a relative in need of help.

One of those people was William T. Hornaday. In 1882, after gaining an extensive education and traveling the world to study animals, Hornaday was put in charge of the Smithsonian Museum's taxidermy collection. In those days taxidermy was considered not odd or ghoulish but a legitimate form of scientific study that not only cataloged species according to their skins but also was part of the education of young boys of the upper classes. It was (and indeed still is) often the gateway drug to illustrious careers in science. Hornaday had always admired buffalo, and he took his job very seriously. In 1886 he became concerned about the reported demise of the great herds and took an inventory of the Smithsonian's buffalo collection. He was startled to find only a few ratty skins and incomplete skeletons— the Smithsonian Institution, the national museum of the United States, did not possess even enough buffalo parts to gather basic scientific data about American's most interesting and iconic mammal, which, less than a century before, had roamed the continent in the tens of millions. Hornaday set the wheels in motion to go to the plains and gather enough skins, skulls, and skeletons to ensure that there was a repository for study.

A few months later, in the first part of May, he found himself in Miles City, Montana, which was the center of the last buffalo range. He was not far from where Theodore Roosevelt had collected his buffalo a few years before. He and his men set up camp in the most likely place—the plateau between the Yellowstone and the Missouri Rivers. It was rough country, difficult for horses, and a perfect place for buffalo to hide from humanity. For four weeks they rode a thoughtful grid but collected only three buffalo, whose thin, ratty summer hides were not good for taxidermy. Hornaday returned to Washington D C to report that the trip had been a bust but he had heard tales of a few buffalo farther north of Miles City, in country even rougher than where they had been searching. His superiors agreed that buffalo populations might be in worse shape than they had thought and they allowed him to return.

On September 24 he was back in Miles City and pushed his team, supplemented by a few local cowboys hired as hunters and guides, to the north. They made camp where Hornaday had heard there were still some buffalo, but for over two weeks they rode their transects without seeing a single buffalo. On the eighteenth day of the expedition one of the cowboys saw a buffalo and fired—apparently he was more cowboy than hunter, because he missed. But Hornaday and his men picked up the trail and began to find a few more buffalo. After two months of hard hunting they finally bagged a total of twenty five—an average day for the hide hunters of just a decade before.

One of the animals was an old bull that Hornaday was particularly proud of. He was a good-sized bull, twelve or fourteen years old, and so was a particular rarity in those last days of the free-roamers—in those days few buffalo lived long enough to grow to full size. In fact, most of the older bulls in the twenty-five Hornaday took from Montana were carrying bullets from previous run-ins with humans. They found old bullets lodged in meat and bones, healed over and testimony to what those last desperate years were like. But the most telling story of

Hornaday's buffalo hunt concerned an even larger bull that they had to chase for twelve grueling miles before he succumbed to their onslaught of bullets. Cruel as that hunt was, Hornaday was elated by such a prize. The long chase had taken up most of the day and they could not finish the skinning and butchering before dark so they retreated to camp for the night.

They set out from camp early the next morning in a wagon, ready to finish the precise job of preparing the head, hide, and skeleton for the first-class taxidermy to be carried out back in Washington D C. When they got to the bull, they found that they were too late. A group of Indians had likely been watching as these white men chased the old bull through the same badlands the Indians had been using as a hideout. They had finished the butchering for Hornaday but they had taken the meat and the hide. As for the skeleton, they had cracked the bones to suck out the marrow. They left the head after taking the tongue and, to Hornaday's disgust, had ruined the fur by smearing the hair on one side with red paint and the other side with yellow. There was also a strip of red flannel tied to one horn.

Hornaday did not speculate on the smears of red and yellow paint. He did not bother to record the orientation to the east or west. He did comment on the strip of red flannel, calling it a signal of defiance. There are other possible interpretations, but he was only a nineteenth-century scientist and not able to understand the reality of those Montana badlands. But despite his shortcomings and the irony of his killing some of the last buffalo, William T. Hornaday was a good man, and after his second trip to the northern buffalo range he understood one important thing: the buffalo were on the brink of extinction and he was in a unique position to help stop that slide into oblivion.

Hornaday went back to Washington and created an exhibit of Great Plains wildlife centered on the buffalo he had collected in Montana. By all accounts the diorama he created was inspiring and created a stir in East Coast society. It almost certainly engendered pangs of guilt and longing in all who saw it. A *Washington Star* reporter described it this way: "A scene from Montana—six of Mr. Hornaday's buffaloes from a picturesque group—a bit of the wild west reproduced at the National Museum—something novel in the way of taxidermy—real buffalo grass, real Montana dirt and real buffalos."

It is unclear whether Harold Baynes saw Hornaday's exhibit, but he certainly heard about it. He was a naturalist and a journalist with a healthy curiosity and energy to burn. In 1904 he moved to a property in New Hampshire that bordered the private game preserve of a railroad tycoon named Austin Corbin, who had acquired some of Buffalo Jones's buffalo when Jones had to sell them to make ends meet out in Kansas. They were the nucleus of Corbin's herd, which had grown to about 160 animals. Bayes fell in love with Corbin's buffalo just about the time Corbin died, and when the heirs threatened to disperse the herd because the cost of its upkeep was too much, he went to work to save it.

Baynes calculated that, at that time, there were about seven hundred buffalo in private hands and they were the majority of the buffalo remaining in the world. He figured that those private herds would eventually face the same sad fate as Corbin's herd—divided up and sold to the highest bidder. He wrote a series of articles for the *Boston Evening Transcript* about buffalo in general and the plight of private herds in particular. Baynes proposed that no individual could assure the care of a herd of buffalo in perpetuity and suggested that the federal government take charge of the conservation of the American buffalo. He made it perfectly clear that buffalo were in immediate peril of extinction and that all Americans were culpable. He insisted that it was now or never. The response to those articles was strong enough to inspire Baynes to undertake a one-man letter-writing campaign to reach influential individuals who might be inclined to lend their voices and their dollars to the cause. After a hundred years of horrible treatment and appalling luck, the buffalo finally got a break. One of those letters made its way to the desk of the president of the United States, Theodore Roosevelt.

Few men were more understanding of the situation of the Great Plains and the plight of the buffalo than Roosevelt. No previous president (or president that followed) had more of a grasp of what extinction actually meant, and in 1905 no man was more powerful. Roosevelt's response to the unsolicited letter from a small-time journalist was straightforward, clear, and powerful: "I am much impressed with your letter, and I agree with every word you say." In his letter back to Roosevelt, Baynes told the president of his idea of creating national preserves for the buffalo. It was not a new idea to Roosevelt, but when Baynes mentioned a specific herd, on the Flathead Reservation, that was for sale and about to be lost to the Canadian government, Roosevelt told Baynes that the plight of the buffalo was of enough importance to be mentioned in his annual State of the Union address. On December 5, 1905, addressing both houses of Congress, Roosevelt put the restoration of the American buffalo on the national agenda: "The most characteristic animal of the western plains was the great shaggy-maned wild ox, the bison, commonly known as buffalo. Small fragments of the herds exist in a domestic state, here and there, a few of them in Yellowstone Park. Such a herd as that on the Flathead Reservation should not be allowed to go out of existence. Either on some reservation or on some forest reserve like the Wichita Reserve or some refuge, provision should be made for preservation of such a herd."

The herd that Roosevelt was referring to was, of course, the herd of Michel Pablo—the herd that was generated from the small group of calves that Samuel Walking Coyote and his wife had brought from the Great Plains back to the Flathead Reservation. Roosevelt's appeal to the U.S. Congress for funding was ignored but his speech created great interest in buffalo, and passion for their conservation soared. So much so that Baynes hit the road on a lecture tour. From that tour emerged a concrete idea that would set the course of the rest of Baynes's life and for the future of buffalo in America. Baynes returned from his tour with the idea that a group of influential and wealthy people should be gathered to raise money, influence legislation, and in concert with federal and state governments, oversee the establishment of buffalo preserves across the American Great Plains. The name of the group would be the American Bison Society. The membership would be exclusive, with William T. Hornaday serving as president, Harold Baynes as secretary, and Theodore Roosevelt as honorary president. They first meet on December 8, 1905, in the Lion House at the New York Zoological Park, where Hornaday was, by then, director.

The society's membership rose quickly to several hundred, mostly from the East Coast. Everyone paid reasonable dues, but fourteen men did most of the work in the early years. Of those fourteen, all but four lived in New York, and only one, Buffalo Jones, lived on the Great Plains. In 1905, when the American Bison Society was founded, the U.S. government was the caretaker of less than a hundred buffalo.

Hornaday and company went to work and found buffalo to populate the National Wichita Forest Reserve in Oklahoma and pushed for legislation to establish the National Bison Range in Montana. They hoped to stock this new federal range with buffalo through purchase of the herd from the Flathead Reservation that Roosevelt had mentioned in his State of the Union address, but to the great embarrassment of Congress, who had dragged their feet on the purchase, the herd went to Canada.

But the American Bison Society raised the money and found other buffalo. By the autumn of 1909 the U.S. government owned 158 buffalo: 7 in the National Zoological Park in Washington DC, about 95 in Yellowstone National Park, 19 on the Wichita Game Reserve in Oklahoma, and 37 on the National Bison Range in Montana. Compared to what the government had been responsible for after the Louisiana Purchase, it was a pitifully small number of animals on a postage stamp of land. But it was a first step on a symbolic journey back toward the dignity that had been stolen with unparalleled brutality and greed.

The American Bison Society went on to help establish national herds at Fort Niobrara Reserve in Nebraska, Wind Cave National Park in South Dakota, and the ironically named Custer State Park—also in South Dakota. By the 1930s, when the society became inactive, it had helped push the number of buffalo to over twenty thousand. Even though more buffalo were still owned by private individuals than by government entities, the society had done what it had set out to do. It had, in a sense, saved the buffalo from extinction. But, as is the flaw of most conservation efforts focused on a single species, society members did not think much about what it really meant to be a buffalo. Understanding of the vital link between a species and its environment continued to elude most of the best conservationists of the era. While the American Bison Society was working to make sure that the species did not blink out forever, immense forces were conspiring to make sure they never roamed their kingdom again, and the humiliation and abuse of the buffalo continued.

Scattered across America and Canada were men and government agencies intent on domesticating the buffalo. Many attempts were made to "break" buffalo to be ridden or to pull carts like draft horses or oxen. While these attempts would eventually fail, the promoters of such ideas predicted fortunes for those who would join in these efforts. It is understandable that a man with Buffalo Jones's entrepreneurial proclivities would endorse a scheme to enlist buffalo to participate in the same juggernaut that destroyed their dominance of the Great Plains, but other, more principled Americans, such as Charles Goodnight and Harold Baynes, were proponents, too.

For most of their history, the relationship between men and buffalo has been grounded in man's desire and need to use parts of buffalo for shelter and food—traded by the buffalo for man's respect for buffalo and their habitat. It was a spiritual bargain, and only when man gave into his attraction for base exploitation did that relationship come off the rails. We are now nearing the end of that period of ruthless exploitation and, ironically, man's old desire and need to eat buffalo meat is proving to be the main driving force for the buffalo's resurgence in numbers. We can only hope that spiritual respect for the buffalo will soon follow.

Since 1888, surveys of buffalo numbers have been taken by various means. The accuracy of these surveys is difficult to judge, but from these records it is reasonable to state that from thirty million to forty million in precontact days, the buffalo's numbers fell steadily until about 1895, when, according to Ernest Thompson Seton's survey, the number bottomed out at eight hundred individuals. From that low point, the numbers climbed slowly but steadily to a little over thirty thousand in the 1970s. It is interesting to note that it was in the late 1970s and early 1980s that buffalo meat was rediscovered as a very healthy and tasty source of protein. That discovery reinstated the vital link between buffalo and humans and elevated their importance beyond that of a mere curiosity. As a result, the continent-wide population of buffalo leaped to over five hundred thousand. This appears to be a success story, but when it comes to buffalo, mere numbers do not tell the whole story.

CHAPTER NINE

Legacy

Lessons from the Buffalo

The buffalo of the Great Plains have shown us that single-species conservation is no real conservation at all. One species can't be separated from the myriad species that make up an ecosystem without significantly changing that ecosystem. The removal of any species sends shockwaves through the entire ecosystem. Sometimes those shockwaves are subtle and hardly noticed. At other times the effects of an extinction are blatantly obvious, with immediate and permanent effect. Buffalo fall into the second category. Though their extinction was never complete, over most of their range buffalo have been missing from the ecosystem since the late nineteenth century. The effect has become systemic: the landscape has not recovered. Additional assaults to the plant and animal communities from other human activities have made any grand recovery of the Great Plains ecosystem unlikely.

With their powers of invention, humans have forever changed the buffalo kingdom. Some of the changes have probably been good and others have probably been bad. They have almost all been extraordinary, but most have been woefully shortsighted. My cousin was a philosophy professor at Brandeis University, and forty-five years ago we had a discussion that I have never forgotten. He was fifteen years older than I was, a Harvard graduate with a PhD in the philosophy of science. He would go on to be the first person I ever met who had actually written a book. I was a young, idealistic graduate student who was more interested in bird watching than understanding esoteric ideas and the study of knowledge. Still, I remember the discussion as being one of the most provoking of my life.

He was in the middle of a life crisis, the details of which I cannot now remember, and had driven to South Dakota to hang out with me and clear his head. Of course, we'd been drinking whiskey for most of the night, and when the good-natured banter got around to the uses of natural resources and our responsibilities to other species I was passionate but tremendously outgunned. This was in the early 1970s, and much of what we were talking about was just coming into the national debate. *Silent Spring* was already ten years old, but I had just read it.

I can't remember what I was responding to but I do remember protesting earnestly that "birds need a place to live too." My cousin looked at me and smiled—not unkindly, but professorially. "There are no needs," he said, "except human needs." I was struck dumb. I stared at him, then let my eyes drift to the window where the sun was just coming up. I knew what he was getting at: the whole concept of need is a human construct; other species have no facility to process the idea. "Only humans have needs." Of course, most people understand the statement to be true, but it did not seem true to me then and it still doesn't. That night I was incapable of responding. But I've been thinking about that night for forty-five years and wish I could replay it, because I now know what I would say. If I had it to do over again I would calmly look back from that pink morning sky, meet my cousin's gaze, and say, "You are wrong. Just like humans, the birds, animals, and maybe even plants have needs. Their needs are our needs. All needs are the same. Maybe there is only one need."

There was nothing hateful or evil in my cousin's reading of the relationship between men and nature. Like the vast majority of mankind in recent years, and perhaps forever, he was simply indoctrinated with an anthropocentric worldview.

On our ranch here in South Dakota, we harvest the buffalo in the same pastures they were born in. There is no confinement feeding, only native grass, pure water, and sunshine to nourish them. We do not cull the old animals, load them into trucks, and send them off to slaughter plants to receive a salvage price. We let those old grandmothers continue to lead their daughters and granddaughters, and indeed the whole herd, to the hard-to-find springs in our winter pastures. They are the first to jump into the icy water of the Cheyenne River when it is time to return to the calving pastures. We let them die out on those pastures that have been their home since they were calves. Since there are no wolves or grizzly bears left in South Dakota, we mimic their role in the ecosystem and put a kindly bullet in the heads of animals that become too weak to move with the herd. We let the carcasses lay where they drop. I have been accused of being wasteful, but in my view, nothing is wasted. Indeed, eagles, coyotes, vultures, crows, swift foxes, mountain lions, maggots, and the microbes of the soil need food too.

In the anthropocentric view, man comes first, and that would be a reasonable stance if men were like other animals and couldn't reason. But that view also holds that men can indeed reason, and that is the main thing that separates them from other animals. The anthropocentric view smacks of having it both ways. But even if the most important question to be answered is "What is in the best interest of humanity?," it cannot be considered in the short term, and so degrading the ecosystem from which we arose cannot be the best answer.

The buffalo's relationship to men may no longer be one of symbiotic support—a tradeoff of food, shelter, and tools from one party for the simple respect of the other party. This notion, for all its appeal, does in fact seem primitive and overly romantic to us modern men. In the twenty-first century, for at least some of us, our gift to the buffalo remains the same; the buffalo's gifts to us have changed.

Of all humanity's clever tools, perhaps the greatest is metaphor. Buffalo can serve as the metaphor for all wildness, and the lesson in their near extinction and return can inform us all about bringing our planet back to balance. Even from their diminished place in the world, the idea of buffalo and the ecosystem they are a part of remain a powerful force in the new era, dominated by human beings and their acquisitive ways. Because during those near-extinction times Europeans and immigrant Americans saw buffalo only as a resource to be exploited, no one paid much attention to their behavior and few understood the buffalo's spiritual value to mankind. Only in recent times have buffalo been studied and considered, both behaviorally and spiritually. Glimpses of understanding are beginning to emerge. Ranchers and land mangers across the Great Plains are experimenting with progressive business models.

Throughout my life I have enjoyed a relationship with peregrine falcons. I have hunted with them on the Great Plains for nearly fifty years and have traveled a great portion of the world studying them from the top of massive cliffs and on long, lonely white-sand beaches. When I describe a peregrine falcon to someone who has never seen one, I begin with, "When they shoot over your head at an altitude of a thousand feet, they look like a tiny black anchor, a meteorite, a cannonball shot from God's own cannon." I do not bother with the subtleties of their plumage or the length of their wings or the color of their feet. I begin with what defines them best—their powers of flight. A peregrine falcon with a broken wing is no peregrine at all. A cage full of such birds tells you almost nothing. It is the same with buffalo—a buffalo that does not move at least a few miles per day is not a buffalo. A buffalo that eats anything but grass is not a buffalo. A buffalo that does not spend its whole life bonded to a familiar herd is not a buffalo.

Regretfully, the buffalo of today's world are no longer wild, but they can still be buffalo. They are owned by conservation groups, the National Park Service, zoos, Ted Turner, Indian tribes, and small, private ranchers like us. Almost all of these people and entities exploit the romance and special place that buffalo hold in the American psyche. They profess a love and respect for buffalo, but the test of that love and respect depends on allowing the buffalo to be real buffalo. In most cases, modern buffalo are no more real buffalo than that peregrine falcon with a broken wing is a real peregrine falcon. Almost always, once the buffalo owned by these people or entities have been exploited for their value as icons, they are forced into corrals, separated from their herds, loaded roughly into noisy, clattering semitrucks, and hauled off to feedlots, where they are fattened beyond what is normal on a diet of subsidized, GMO grains. They are then hauled off to modern slaughter plants where they finally face the heart of industrial meat production in the form of white-coated butchers operating gleaming stainless steel machinery. They are forced into chutes and held tight while low-paid employees hold bolt guns against their heads and pull the triggers.

Death is something that we all must come to terms with. The fact that we all must die is not in dispute and not necessarily odious. How we die is another matter. Honor and respect should be afforded to all of us. But even more important than how we die is how we live. If we are indeed brothers of the buffalo, it is a Cain and Abel relationship. At every turn modern humans have tried to destroy their brothers. It is as if we are jealous of the buffalo—their freedom of movement, their power, the ease with which they fit into their environment.

Even the institutions that claim to have the buffalo's best interests at heart seem not to understand their true nature and appear to be plotting against them. With honest intentions, humans try to protect buffalo from what we fear. We want our buffalo on rolling hills of grass that are never dry. We want our buffalo to be warm in winter and cool in summer. We want to view them in snapshots of pristine nature. We want them behind fences where they are controlled, and sadly, that is where they must be. We want them protected from wolves and grizzly bears and spring floods and monster blizzards. When they overpopulate their range we want part of the herd to magically disappear to make room for more cute golden babies in the spring. We try not to think of where they go when they disappear. The conservation groups, National Park Service, and large private herd owners are masters of this great disappearing act. While claiming to honor what is best for the buffalo they have become addicted to the image and association with buffalo. Their buffalo have become an economic driver of their private fiefdoms. To improve their bottom lines and to make room for the yearly regeneration of a given herd, they separate the calves from their herds, crowd them into those semitrucks, and ship them off to the feedlots as if they were merely cattle. The responsibility to treat buffalo like relatives ends when the trucks leave the property. People pat themselves on the back and send out another press release talking about their deep commitment to conservation, and no one thinks about what it means to a buffalo to spend its last year of life in confinement—breathing the toxic fumes from the feedlot and waiting for the end.

Of course, the culpable institutions try to put a happy face on what they are doing. Some of the buffalo are given to Indian tribes, which sounds good but, in reality, only means that the buffalo are hauled from one set of corrals to the next, banged around in trucks and squeeze chutes, injured and sometimes accidentally killed. Finally they end up in filthy feedlots. There they face months of confinement, no movement, nothing green. To be treated like cattle is perhaps the greatest humiliation of their long history of abuse at the hands of industrial man.

This is what I see when I travel the Great Plains. I am no tree hugger. I'm a hunter and a carnivore who lives in the real world. I could accept the feedlots and industrial agriculture if it was as simple as my own survival and the survival of my family. But it is not that simple. The people and institutions that indulge in the industrialization of buffalo while hiding behind tired slogans like "We're feeding the world," "We're saving the buffalo," or "We're giving the people what they want" are actually only the latest version of buffalo exploitation. By confining buffalo in feedlots, particularly where G M O crops are used to layer on the fat, our culture is only perpetuating the destruction of the buffalo and the Great Plains by encouraging the conversion of biodiverse grasslands to sterile, monoculture crop production. Forcing buffalo to participate in this destruction of their own habitat is the final insult. We should be able to do better.

Innovation has been the backbone of man's manic drive for dominance over nature. We are a very smart animal. But in our relationship with buffalo, we display a total lack of imagination. We need to reclaim the creative innovation that makes us human. Certainly we can figure out an honorable model for our ongoing relationship with buffalo and the landscape that gave them life.

APPENDIX

Where to Find Buffalo on the Great Plains

National Parks and Preserves
Badlands National Park, South Dakota
Fort Niobrara, Nebraska
National Bison Range, Montana
Sully Hills National Wildlife Refuge, North Dakota
Theodore Roosevelt National Park, North Dakota
Walnut Creek National Wildlife Refuge, Iowa
Wichita Mountains National Wildlife Refuge, Oklahoma
Wind Cave National Park, South Dakota
Yellowstone National Park, Idaho, Montana, Wyoming

State Parks
Antelope Island State Park, Utah
Blue Mound State Park, Minnesota
Caprock Canyon State Park, Texas
Custer State Park, South Dakota
Elk Island, Alberta
Fort Robinson State Park, Nebraska
Genesee State Park, Colorado

Henry Mountain State Park, Utah

Hot Springs State Park, Wyoming

Maxwell State Game Refuge, Kansas

Minneopa State Park, Minnesota

Prairie State Park, Missouri

Sandsage Bison Range, Kansas

Wildlife Prairie State Park, Illinois

BIBLIOGRAPHY

Brinkley, Douglas. *The Wilderness Warrior: Theodore Roosevelt and the Crusade for America*. New York: HarperCollins, 2009.

Brown, Dee. *Bury My Heart at Wounded Knee: An Indian History of the American West*. Foreword by Hampton Sides. New York: Sterling Innovation, 2009.

Campbell, Ballard C. *Disasters, Accidents, and Crises in American History: A Reference Guide to the Nation's Most Catastrophic Events*. New York: Facts on File, 2008.

Carson, Rachel. *Silent Spring*. Introduction by Al Gore. Drawings by Lois and Louis Darling. Boston: Houghton Mifflin, 1994.

Dana, Richard Henry, Jr. *Two Years Before the Mast: A Personal Narrative of Life at Sea*. Illustrations by E. Boyd Smith. Afterword by Thomas Fleming. Pleasantville NY: Reader's Digest Association, 1995.

Dary, David A. *The Buffalo Book: The Full Saga of the American Animal*. Athens: Swallow Press/Ohio University Press, 1989.

Dinsmore, James J. *A Country So Full of Game: The Story of Wildlife in Iowa*. Illustrated by Mark Miller. Iowa City: University of Iowa Press, 1994.

Hurt, R. Douglas. *The Dust Bowl: An Agricultural and Social History*. Chicago: Nelson-Hall, 1981.

Isenberg, Andrew C. *The Destruction of the Bison: An Environmental History, 1750–1920*. Cambridge: Cambridge University Press, 2000.

Lewis, Meriwether, and William Clark. *The Definitive Journals of Lewis and Clark*. Edited by Gary E. Moulton. 13 vols. Lincoln: University of Nebraska Press, 1983–2004.

Linklater, Andro. *Measuring America: How an Untamed Wilderness Shaped the United States and Fulfilled the Promise of Democracy.* New York: Walker, 2002.

Mann, Charles C. *1491: New Revelations of the Americas before Columbus.* New York: Vintage, 2006.

Manning, Richard. *Against the Grain: How Agriculture Has Hijacked Civilization.* New York: North Point Press, 2014.

McHugh, Tom. *The Time of the Buffalo.* With the assistance of Victoria Hobson. New York: Knopf, 1972.

McMurtry, Larry. *Lonesome Dove: A Novel.* New York: Simon & Schuster, 2010.

Mead, James R. *Hunting and Trading on the Great Plains, 1859–1875.* Edited by Schuyler Jones. Introduction by Ignace Mead Jones. Wichita KS: Rowfant Press, 2008.

Neihardt, John G. *Black Elk Speaks: The Complete Edition.* With a new introduction by Philip J. Deloria and annotations by Raymond J. DeMallie. Lincoln: University of Nebraska Press, 2014.

Piper, Edwin Ford. *Barbed Wire and Wayfarers.* New York: Macmillan, 1924.

Powers, William K. *Oglala Religion.* Lincoln: University of Nebraska Press, 1977.

Roosevelt, Theodore. *Ranch Life and the Hunting Trail.* Illustrated by Frederic Remington. Mineola NY: Dover, 2009.

Snyder, Gerald S. *In the Footsteps of Lewis and Clark.* Photos by Dick Durrance II. Illustrated by Richard Schledcht. Foreword by Donald Jackson. Washington DC: Special Publications Division, National Geographic Society, 1970.

Stegner, Wallace. *Beyond the Hundredth Meridian: John Wesley Powell and the Second Opening of the West.* Introduction by Bernard De Voto. Lincoln: University of Nebraska Press, 1982.

Wallis, George A. *Cattle Kings of the Staked Plains.* Denver: Sage Books, 1964.

Webb, Walter Prescott. *The Great Plains.* Lincoln: University of Nebraska Press, 1981.

INDEX

Italicized page numbers refer to maps, and italicized figure numbers refer to illustrations following page 50.

Adobe Walls, 36
Against the Grain (Manning), 80
agriculture. *See* farming
Allard, Charles, 82
American Bison Society, 92, 93
American Fur Company, 32
Antelope Island State Park, 103
Arapaho, 32, 36, 44, 45
Ashley, William H., 18–19
Astor, John Jacob, *fig. 11*, 18–19, 32
Atlantic, 24

Badlands National Park, 103
barbed wire, 58, 59, 61–62, 63–64
Barnum, P. T., 83
Baynes, Harold, 90–91, 92, 94
beaver pelt trade, 16–17, 19–20, 32
Bering land bridge, *2*, 3–4
biodiversity, 70, 72–73, 78, 79, 101
bison: arrival in Great Plains of,
   2, 3–4; breeding by, 40–41;
   "buffalo" as misnomer for,
xi; calves, *fig. 17*, *fig. 18*, 42,
43; conservationists' effort
to protect, 59–60; docility
of, 5, 61; evolution of, 5, 25;
explorers' observations of,
10–11; grass-eating diet of,
9–10; herds of, 12–13, 15, 43;
horns of, *fig. 15*, *fig. 16*, 42–43;
and horses, 26–30; human
relationship with, 25, 97–98;
Indians' cultural reliance on,
1, 11, 14, 17, 31; as keystone
species, 13–14; and livestock-
borne disease, 18; as metaphor
for wildness, 98; movements
of, 12–13; population figures
for, 11–12, 18, 94; range of, *3*;
rebuilding population of, 81–
94; U.S. Army war on, 34, 47;
as U.S. national mammal, xiii;
during winter, 41–42
bison hides, 29, 30–31, 34, 35

bison hunting: by early hunters and trappers, 15–16; by Indians on horses, 26–30; legislation on, 59, 60; by primitive peoples, 5–7; scavenging animals and, 7, 34–35. *See also* buffalo hunters

bison meat, 11, 37; in Indians' diet, 28; modern resurgence of, 94; trade in, 29, 30, 31, 35

bison robes, 19, 29, 30–31

Black Elk Speaks, 50

Black Hills, xi, 45, 46

Blue Mound State Park, 103

Boone, Daniel, 8

Bosch, Carl, 69–70

Boston Evening Transcript, 90

Bowen, John T., *fig. 4*

Bozeman Trail, 44

Brown, Dee, 50

buffalo hunters: Buffalo Bill Cody, *fig. 14*, 35, 83; on northern range, 39–40; slaughter of millions by, *fig. 9*, 32, 35, 39, 41, 59; on southern plains, 32–33, 34–36; in Texas panhandle, 34, 36; U.S. Army sponsorship of, 34. *See also* bison hunting

Burlington & Missouri River Railroad, *fig. 8*

Bury My Heart at Wounded Knee (Brown), 50

Cabeza de Vaca, Álvar Núñez, 7–8

Campbell, Ballard C., 18

Caprock Canyon State Park, 103

Carson, Rachel, 74

cattle, 37, 53–55, 58

Cheyenne, 32, 36, 44, 45, 47; Sand Creek massacre of, 33

Cheyenne River, *fig. 19*, xii, 49, 97

Chouteau, Pierre, 18–19

Civil War, 32, 43

Cody, William F. "Buffalo Bill," *fig. 14*, 35, 83

Comanche, 29, 36

Conquering Bear, 38, 44

conservation, 25, 56–57, 59–60, 95

Corbin, Austin, 90

Cortés, Hernán, 7

Crazy Horse, 44, 46, 47

Crook, George, 46

Custer, George Armstrong, 33, 45, 46

Custer State Park, 93, 103

DDT, 73–74

de Soto, Hernando, 18

Disasters, Accidents, and Crises in American History (Campbell), 18

disease, 17–18

Dodge City KS, 35

Dupree, Pete, 84–85, 86

Dust Bowl, *fig. 10*, 25, 66–67

The Dust Bowl: An Agricultural and Social History (Hurt), 66–67

Elk Island, 103

European wisent, xi

farming: and crop seeds, 75–76; destruction from plowing

in, 64–66, 78, 79; dryland, 65–66, 72, 77; GMOs used in, 78–79; by homesteaders, 20–22, 52; monoculture, 70, 72–74, 78, 101; yeoman, 21–22

feedlots, *fig. 20*, 76, 99, 100, 101

fee simple ownership, 62, 63

Fetterman Fight, 44

Flathead Reservation, 81, 82, 91, 92

Forest and Stream, 60

Fort Laramie, 38–39, 44, 46

Fort Niobrara, 93, 103

Fort Robinson State Park, 103

Free Soil Party, 20

Gall, 46

Genesee State Park, 103

Ghost Dance, 48–49

Gibbon, John, 46

GMOs, 78–79, 101

Goodnight, Charles, 84–85, 86, 94

Grant, Ulysses S., 47

grasslands, 29, 54; bison contribution to, 13–14; and bison migration, 5, 15; and cattle, 58–59, 76; conversion of to cropland, 64–65, 72, 78, 79, 101

Grattan, John, 38–39

Great Plains: barbed wire enclosures in, 58, 59, 61–62, 63–64; bison as keystone species in, 13–14; cattle herds brought into, 53–55, 58; destruction of natural ecosystem in, 23–24, 58–59, 64–65, 70–80, 93;

droughts in, 66; Dust Bowl in, 25, 66–67; elevation of, 4–5; Europeans' misconceptions about, 68–69; and feedlot industry, 75–77; formation of, 4; homesteading in, 20–22, 52; horses in, 26–30; lack of rainfall in, 9, 22, 57; land ownership in, 62–64; monoculture farming in, 70, 72–74, 78, 101; Ogallala Aquifer underneath, 70–72; precipitation line in, 77–78; railroads' impact on, 22–23, 35, 62; rebuilding bison herds in, 81–94; technology's impact on, 70–80; territory won in Mexican War, 20, 37; U.S. explorations of, 10–11; vegetation of, 9–10; winters in, 41–42

Great Sioux Reservation, 45

Greeley, Horace, 11–12, 25

Haber, Fritz, 69–70

Harper's Weekly, *fig. 7*

Hennepin, Louis, 8

Henry Mountain State Park, 104

High Forehead, 38

Higley, Brewster M., 13

Homestead Act, 20–22

Hornaday, William T., *fig. 13*, 59, 87–90, 92

horses, 26–30

Hot Springs State Park, 104

Howell, Ed, *fig. 6*, 59–60

Hunting and Trading on the Great Plains, 1859–1875 (Mead), 12

Hurt, R. Douglas, 66–67
hybridization, 75–76

Indians: and beaver-pelt trade, 16–17, 19; bison hunting on horseback by, 26–30; cultural relationship to bison by, 1, 11, 14, 17, 31; early explorers' view of, 10; hostilities with buffalo hunters by, 32; impact of diseases on, 17–18; massacres of, 33, 49–50; treaties with, 32, 36, 37, 45; U.S. Army battles with, 38–39, 44–47
insects, 72–74

Jefferson, Thomas, 10, 21
Jones, Charles Jessie "Buffalo," 83–84, 85, 92, 94

Kansas-Pacific Railroad, *fig. 5*
keystone species, 13–14
Kiowa, 33, 36

Lacey, John F., 60
Lakota, 30, 32, 38–39, 44, 45, 47; Wounded Knee massacre of, 49–50
Lame White Man, 46
land ownership, 62–64
Lewis and Clark expedition, 10–11, 21
Lincoln, Abraham, 20
Lisa, Manuel, 18–19
livestock, 18. *See also* cattle

Manning, Richard, 80
Maxwell State Game Refuge, 104

Mead, James, 12
Medicine Lodge Treaty, 36
Mexican-American War, 20, 37
Miniconjou Sioux, 38, 39
Minneopa State Park, 104
monoculture farming, 70, 72–74, 78, 101
Monsanto, 75
Montezuma, 7
Mormons, 37–38
mountain men, 19, 20
Müller, Paul, 73

National Bison Range, 93, 103
National Wichita Forest Reserve, 92
National Zoological Park, 93
Navajos, 29
New York Times, 71
nitrogen fertilizer, 69–70
North American wood buffalo, xi
Northern Pacific Railroad, 45

Ogallala Aquifer, 70–72
Oglala Sioux, 39, 44

Pablo, Michel, 82–83, 91–92
Paiute, 48
peregrine falcons, 98–99
Philips, "Scotty," 86
Pickens, T. Boone, 71, 72
Pine Ridge Reservation, 48, 49
Powder River Country, 44–47
Powell, John Wesley, 24–25
Prairie State Park, 104
precipitation line, 77–78
Pueblo Indians, 29

railroads, 22–23, 35, 62
Red Cloud, 39, 44
robber barons, 24
Rocky Mountains, 4, 9, 12, 45, 66, 86
Roosevelt, Theodore, *fig. 12*, 56–57, 83, 85, 91–92
Roundup, 75, 78

Sand Creek massacre, 33
Sandsage Bison Range, 104
scavengers, animal, 7, 34–35
seeds, crop, 75–76
Seton, Ernest Thompson, 12, 94
Sheridan, Philip, 12, 33, 47
Sherman, William T., 33–34, 47
Silent Spring (Carson), 74, 96
Sitting Bull, 46, 49
Smithsonian Institution, 87
Spanish rule, 7–8
Spotted Tail, 39
Stanley, John Mix, *fig. 3*
Stronghold Table, 50
Sully Hills National Wildlife Refuge, 103

Terry, Alfred, 46
Texas panhandle, 34, 36, 39, 67, 71
Theodore Roosevelt National Park, 103
Thomas, Cyrus, 25
trade: in beaver pelts, 16–17, 19–20, 32; in buffalo hides, 30–31; in horses, 29

Treaty of Fort Laramie, 32, 45
Treaty of Guadalupe Hidalgo, 37
Turner, Ted, 99
Two Moons, 46

U.S. Army: battles with Indians by, 38–39, 44–47; war on bison by, 34, 47

Van Buren, Martin, 20
Vázquez de Coronado, Francisco, 7–8

Walking Coyote, Samuel, 81–82, 86, 92
Walnut Creek National Wildlife Refuge, 103
Washington Star, 90
water, underground, 70–72
weedkillers, 74–75, 78
White Antelope, 33
Wichita Game Reserve, 93
Wichita Mountains National Wildlife Refuge, 103
Wildlife Prairie State Park, 104
Wind Cave National Park, 93, 103
wolves, 34–35, 42
World War I, 66
Wounded Knee massacre, 49–50
Wovoka, 48–49
Wright, Robert, 12

Yellowstone National Park, 59–60, 85, 91, 93, 103

IN THE DISCOVER THE GREAT PLAINS SERIES

Great Plains Geology
R. F. Diffendal Jr.

Great Plains Bison
Dan O'Brien

Great Plains Indians
David J. Wishart

Discover the Great Plains, a series from the Center for Great Plains Studies and the University of Nebraska Press, offers concise introductions to the natural wonders, diverse cultures, history, and contemporary life of the Great Plains. To order or obtain more information on these or other University of Nebraska Press titles, visit nebraskapress.unl.edu.